# RAIL 300

## THE WORLD HIGH SPEED TRAIN RACE

*Murray Hughes*

DAVID & CHARLES
Newton Abbot London North Pomfret (VT)

*Jacket:* A series 100 bullet train awaits the right away from Tokyo Central for its 5 hr 57 min dash to Hakata, 1,069km away. *Author*

To Paul Drew
who set the points
and K who supplied motive power

*British Library Cataloguing in Publication Data*

Hughes, Murray
Rail 300 : the world high speed
train race.
1. High speed ground transportation
—History
I. Title
625.2′662 TF1315

ISBN 0–7153–8963–7



Photoset and printed in Great Britain by
Redwood Burn Limited, Trowbridge, Wiltshire
for David & Charles Publishers plc
Brunel House, Newton Abbot, Devon

Published in the United States of America
by David & Charles Inc
North Pomfret Vermont 05053 USA

# CONTENTS

# INTRODUCTION

This book is about the magic figures on a train's speedometer. Even around 1900 there were claims to the 100mph and 200km/h trophies. Now both speeds are taken for granted, but it is worth recalling that only a dozen railways in the world operate regular services at 100mph or more. Seven of them run trains at 200km/h and two of these exceed that maximum with ceilings of 240 and 270km/h. The world's first regular service at 300km/h, the French TGV-Atlantique, is less than two years away, hence the title of this book *Rail 300*.

The speed landmarks are a confusing mix of kilometres per hour (km/h) and miles per hour (mph). I have chosen to adopt km/h as all the countries concerned use metric units except for Britain and the USA. Rather than constantly interrupt the text with conversions I include here a summary conversion table of those speeds which are most relevant to the story:

| | |
|---|---|
| 100.0km/h: 62.2mph | 250.0km/h: 155.3mph |
| 150.0km/h: 93.2mph | 260.0km/h: 161.6mph |
| 160.9km/h: 100.0mph | 270.0km/h: 167.8mph |
| 177.0km/h: 110.0mph | 300.0km/h: 186.4mph |
| 200.0km/h: 124.3mph | 321.9km/h: 200.0mph |
| 225.0km/h: 139.8mph | 350.0km/h: 217.5mph |
| 241.4km/h: 150.0mph | 400.0km/h: 248.5mph |

It is usual to equate 100mph with 160km/h, 125mph with 200km/h and 140mph with 225km/h.

Another choice was millions or billions. The continental billion (a thousand million) is now commonly accepted, and I have used this rather than resort to strings of zeros for the yen of Japan and the lire of Italy, both countries where millionaires are two a penny.

Much of the material for this book has been drawn from *Railway Gazette International*, which is a trade paper for railway management and the world's railway industry; it cannot be obtained over the counter at newsagents. Having watched the story of high speed railways unfold in its pages, I felt it was high time that it was told again for all those who follow the modern history of railways. *Railway Gazette* can be obtained by subscription from Reed Publishing, Oakfield House, Perrymount Road, Haywards Heath, Sussex RH16 3DH, England. Another important source was the lively French journal *La Vie du Rail*.

It remains for me to thank all those people who have helped me. Special thanks must go to the other members of the *Railway Gazette* editorial team – Editor Richard Hope for making useful additions to the text and for writing the Foreword. Production Editor Chris Jackson deserves thanks for long-standing support and for spotting some howlers. Thanks also to Jean-Paul Masse of *La Vie du Rail*, to Yves Desailly of the French Railways press office in Paris, and to Mr Takao Takada for his enormous help when I visited Japan. Mr Simon Halewood of the Japan National Tourist Organisation in London has asked me to point out that for anyone wishing to visit the Tokaido shinkansen – without doubt the world's premier high speed inter-city railway, with an incredible *minimum* interval between services of just 12min – that the Japan Rail Pass is still available, despite abolition of Japanese National Railways on 1 April 1987.

I must also acknowledge the assistance of Peter Semmens, formerly Assistant Keeper of the National Railway Museum in York, England, who kindly vetted the table of records forming the Appendix. Peter is a professional speed recorder and writes a monthly article on locomotive practice and performance in *Railway Magazine*, sister of *Railway Gazette*. Thanks also to the staff of Baines Bookshop, Sutton, for help and encouragement, to Mike Barlow, Ralf Roman Rossberg and numerous others.

My most grateful thanks are reserved for my wife who drew nine maps and diagrams and sustained me during my labours at the word processor. Last, a special thank you to my mother who contributed in a most generous way.

Murray Hughes
Assistant Editor *Railway Gazette International*

October 1987

# FOREWORD

## RICHARD HOPE
## Editor of *Railway Gazette International*

Back in 1957, while doing my National Service in the Royal Air Force, one of my fellow officers announced that the passenger train was doomed. I took issue, and bet him £10 that 30 years hence there would still be two daily trains between London and York.

I had to make a trip to Palmerston North in New Zealand in 1987 to collect my money, sadly attenuated by inflation, but at least there was no doubt who had won. Some 25 trains a day speed north from Kings Cross to York, the fastest covering the 302km at an average speed of 152km/h. If the passenger train is an endangered species in New Zealand, it is not so in Europe.

There is a sense, though, in which events proved him right. In 1987 the British Junior Chamber – a training ground for up and coming business executives – decided to hold its annual conference in Belfast. A ship was chartered from Liverpool for delegates from mainland Britain, and the regional committee was asked to investigate secure parking in that city.

Here was a case where driving to Liverpool seemingly offered no advantage, yet the possibility that members might leave their cars at home and travel to Liverpool by train was not even mentioned, let alone seriously considered as an alternative to an inconvenient and no doubt costly parking problem.

For the majority of Britons outside the London area – and many within it – the only forms of transport which exist today are the car and the aeroplane. They have no conception of what modern train travel is like, nor the advantages it offers in terms of speed, comfort and convenience. And it has to be admitted that there is nowhere in Britain, except perhaps central London, from which Liverpool can be reached more quickly by rail than road, given the network of motorways on which it is possible to average 120km/h in the sort of company owned cars favoured by junior executives.

The German Federal Railway, which has lost out badly to the airlines and *Autobahnen*, has coined a slogan: half as fast as the plane, twice as fast as the car.

Thanks to the inconvenient location of airports, and the time taken to get on and off the plane, trains running at half the speed of an Airbus can compete quite effectively for inter-city journeys up to around three hours.

With the car the tables are turned, for now it is the train that is inconvenient. To offset the delays involved in getting to and from the station and waiting for the train, it is necessary to cruise twice as fast as the car for at least an hour, say 200km/h as a minimum.

If the inter-city passenger train is ever to become anything more than a poor relation in the eyes of the majority of travellers who just want to get from one place to another as quickly as possible in reasonable comfort, maximum speeds must be lifted into the 200 to 300km/h range. It is a question of survival.

It did not look that way in October 1964 when Japanese National Railways (JNR) launched the world's first scheduled service exceeding 160km/h and known as the shinkansen; capacity to cope with burgeoning demand was the driving force. But the shinkansen may yet prove as significant a development for passenger railways as the appearance of commercial jets was for civil aviation a decade earlier.

As it happens, the 23 years that have elapsed since JNR first breached the 200km/h barrier coincide almost exactly with my time on the editorial staff of *Railway Gazette*. In the front line trenches of journalism, it is easy to become so engrossed in the growth of individual trees that one has to step back a pace to appreciate the shape of the wood.

Herein lies the value of an authoritative work such as *Rail 300 – The World High Speed Train Race*. Murray Hughes has skilfully teased out the important strands of a very complex tale, which has seen many setbacks and disappointments such as Penn Central's *Metroliners* and British Rail's ill-fated APT, as well as remarkable success stories like the TGV.

Having followed all of these sagas month by month, rejoicing in victory and commiserating with defeat, it is fascinating to read such a comprehensive overview – which incidentally includes many nuggets of information which were denied to us at the time.

Two questions remain; how fast will trains run in the years ahead, and how many high speed lines will actually get built?

The first is perhaps the easiest to answer. No matter how smooth or energy-efficient the support and guidance system, there are fundamental restraints on the speed which can be economically justified at ground level when competing with aircraft flying 8km high where the air is much thinner and there is less resistance to forward motion. The power needed to force any train through the atmosphere rises as the square of the speed. Above 200km/h, aerodynamic resistance absorbs most of the traction energy needed to sustain forward motion.

There is also the problem of finding an acceptable route through the world's most crowded and highly developed regions, for where else can sufficient traffic be found? As speed rises, curves must be of larger radius to keep forces within acceptable limits, noise becomes more of a problem, and the economic penalties of adding stops to serve intermediate towns – a major advantage which the train normally enjoys over the plane – rise sharply.

Some calculations have been done which put the maximum economic speed for trains between 250 and 300km/h. Technical advances, for example in reducing aerodynamic drag, will probably lift the upper end of the range to 350 or perhaps even 400km/h eventually, but the limit is there and magnetic levitation does nothing to overcome it.

It is much harder to say where new high speed lines will be built. There is no doubt that the Tokaido shinkansen and Paris–Sud-Est lines are profitable in the strictest commercial sense, but the same is unlikely to be true of shinkansen lines to Sapporo and Nagasaki. It seems that a minimum of 10 million passengers a year is needed to break even, and it is far from obvious where that kind of traffic is going to come from between Sydney and Melbourne, for instance.

In North America, where the demography is right in half-a-dozen corridors, there is likely to be a major problem in attracting sufficient passengers because the highly developed feeder network of local trains and buses found in Europe or Japan does not exist – or not in a socially acceptable form, at least.

But if the high speed train is not destined to become a universal transport mode like the ubiquitous jet plane, it certainly has all the makings of a success story in specific locations. The real turning point will come when governments tire of duplicating clogged motorways and trying to shoehorn more short-haul planes into existing airports, as is happening in the Washington–Boston Northeast Corridor.

Once high speed lines are assessed on an equal basis with investment in other modes, instead of being judged on narrow financial criteria, new construction may dwarf anything that we have seen up to now. It will be time for Volume II.

# 1
# THE RECORD BREAKERS

Early in the afternoon of 25 February 1981 Jean Dupuy, then deputy general-manager of French National Railways (SNCF), boarded a train in a remote part of central France. The train made six short runs with Dupuy on board. After the sixth he gave the all-clear to proceed with the programme. During the evening the telephones rang in the Paris newsrooms, and duty editors noted the rendezvous for the next day, 26 February.

Back on the line, railway staff made the final preparations for the following day's event. These included changing the number of the set forming the special train from 33 back to its real number of 16. A disguise had been necessary to divert the attention of the curious in the elaborate build up to the operation. Codenamed Antilope, or officially TGV 100, it signified an attempt to accelerate a train up to the staggering speed of 100 metres/sec, which is 6km a minute or 360km/h.

Set 16 was no ordinary train. It was the pick of SNCF's fleet of brand new *Trains à Grande Vitesse* (TGV). It had been chosen before its birth as the instrument for the test and was specially manicured for the occasion. On 25 February, with Dupuy on board, it had twice achieved the 100 metres/sec objective, becoming the fastest train in the world. The next day Dupuy would decide just how far past that mark they dare go.

In the afternoon of 26 February about 100 journalists, radio and TV crews had arrived and were in position by 15.00. At 15.28 Jean-Marie Metzler, head of the test team on board the train, gave the word for departure. With him in the second coach of the seven-car set, transformed into a rolling laboratory crammed with electronics and sophisticated recording gear, was SNCF's deputy rolling stock director Raymond Garde. Esconced in the leading cab was Dupuy, drivers Gabriel Jacquot and Henri Dejeux, rolling stock design engineer André Cossié and one guest, none other than Fernand Nouvion.

Nouvion was no stranger to world records. He it was who as deputy chief of SNCF's electric traction research division had engineered the dramatic French trials of 1955, when two locomotives had pioneered a world rail speed record that had stood untouched for 26 years.

The 1955 trials were a deliberate attempt to push traction and track to the ultimate limit. SNCF had been encouraged by the success of five days of trials in February 1954 with an unmodified six-axle locomotive (No CC7121), hauling three coaches during which 243km/h was attained at Vougeot between Dijon and Beaune on the Paris–Lyons main line, newly electrified in 1952. In 1955 it set out to better the achievement. The test ground selected was the Lamothe–Morcenx section of the Bordeaux–Hendaye main line, flat and dead straight apart from a single curve of 3,700 metres radius at one end.

With the help of two mobile substations borrowed from the Paris–Lyons line the dc traction supply to the catenary was boosted from 1.5 to 1.9kV. Two locomotives were picked for the attempt, the four-axle BB9004 and the six-axle CC7107; both were regeared and fitted with monobloc wheels and special pantographs. The test train was formed of three third class cars with rubber fairings between them and an aerodynamically rounded tail section with observation window.

A series of preliminary runs completed the preparations and on 26 March the BB hurtled up to 276km/h, a new world record. By this time word about the tests had got around, and two days later found quite a crowd gathered at Ychoux, the spot where maximum speed was likely to be reached. Level crossings along the route were closed and guarded by gendarmes. Those who had heeded the rumours were not disappointed. In the early afternoon CC7107 rocketed through Ychoux in a dramatic run that smashed the 300km/h barrier and saw a pantograph dissolve into strips of red-hot metal, setting trackside pine trees alight. But SNCF did not reveal the exact speed that had been attained.

Next day it was the turn of the BB again. In an even more sensational dash the machine powered up to whirlwind speed, and once more a pantograph melted in an explosive burst of purple arcing. The train roared through Ychoux, leaving behind a cloud of dust and a hail of flying ballast flung up by the slipstream. After the run, SNCF announced that both the BB and CC locomotives had attained the staggering maximum of 331km/h.

While no-one disputed that this fantastic speed had been reached, there was some doubt cast in the British press that both locomotives should have attained precisely the same maximum, but SNCF maintained officially that they had. Not until 31 years had passed and a new record was safely in the bag did the French reveal* that the 331km/h had only been attained by the BB.

The CC, it turned out, had reached 326km/h – still a quite remarkable achievement – but it had been agreed by the parties concerned, in deference to the two manufacturers, Alsthom for the CC and MTE for the BB, that if the difference in maximum speed was only around 5km/h the highest speed would be cited for both machines. Given the difficulties of recording the exact speed and possible variations in power supply, the decision was understandable. But the French are past masters at publicity and keeping secrets.

Only in 1981 did it become public knowledge that BB9004's staggering record had come within a hair's breadth of disaster. During the run a bout of vicious hunting broke out, with the thrashing side to side movement of the bogies exerting such tremendous lateral force on the track that the rails were distorted into serpent-like strings that looked barely fit for any train to pass over them without derailing.

In February 1981 SNCF could not afford to take technical risks – it was only seven months away from launching regular services at 260km/h on the first part of a spanking new railway between Paris and Lyons.

It was on a completed section of this new railway, the Paris–Sud-Est line, that TGV set 16 responded to Metzler's signal to move. On reaching the specially prepared test section, the streaking train was already a blur of orange, white and grey as it thundered past lineside observers at 340km/h. Over the next 13km the standard 120mm$^2$ contact wire had been replaced by a 150mm$^2$ strand, and the tension had been increased from 15 to 20kN. To provide extra power the voltage had been boosted from 25 to 30kV.

As the train flashed into the test section, Metzler was checking by radio with lineside staff that nothing obstructed the track ahead (in an earlier test a photographer had stepped too near the track, resulting in an emergency brake application at over 330km/h).

All was clear, and Set 16 surged on at full power. About 7km into the test section speed was 370km/h, and still the train accelerated. At 15.41, Dupuy gave the command to cut traction. The train was powering along at a fraction over 380km/h, and the name of Moulins-

* *Histoire de la Traction Electrique*, Vol 2, by Yves Machefert-Tassin, Fernand Nouvion and Jean Woimant. Editions La Vie du Rail, 11 rue de Milan, 75440 Paris Cedex 09, France.

Close to disaster. Just how near the French BB9004 locomotive came to catastrophe when it achieved the 1955 world record of 331km/h was a closely guarded secret until this photograph – not published until 1981 – revealed the extent of track deformation. *La Vie du Rail*

en-Tonnerrois where this speed had been attained was grafted into the annals of railway history.

Dupuy's decision to go no faster was occasioned by aerodynamic uplift of the two-stage pantograph – the maximum uplift commensurate with safety was 250mm, and at Moulins the lift was already 230mm. According to Dupuy, no other technical limit had been approached.

The waiting journalists were then invited on board the record-breaker which minutes before had blasted past them on its historic run. This time the driver reined in at 364km/h, but it was enough. Next day the French newspapers hailed the achievement with such headlines as 'Fabulous TGV'. Telegrams arrived from French President Giscard d'Estaing and Prime Minister Raymond Barre. Dupuy insisted that the time would come when SNCF would go even faster.

The decision to go for the record had been taken over a year before, on 15 February 1980. Set 16 was due out of the builders' shops in October that year. It was not a standard TGV as it only had seven cars, three having been set aside to ensure a high power to weight ratio. With 10,000kW available on the test section, the total weight was only 307 tonnes. All the powered axles were fitted with wheels of 1,050mm diameter instead of the standard 920mm; the gear ratio was altered too. Before the trials as many components as possible had been put through a programme of static tests at SNCF's Vitry laboratory.

The TGV record has stood unequalled for seven years, confirming SNCF's position as king of the league table of world record runs. The French have held the world record for 33 years, and only one other country has shared that honour since the turn of the century.

There was, however, a run at 410km/h on 14 August 1974 by an American research vehicle powered by jet engines as well as gas turbines feeding a linear motor. This was purely an experimental vehicle with no passenger accommodation, but it did run on standard gauge track (Chapter 6). Strictly speaking, therefore, this holds the absolute world rail speed record – but it may well be that a TGV beats it in the next two or three years.

Before France's 1954 record of 243km/h the blue riband belonged to Germany, which had reached 230km/h back in 1931 with one of the strangest vehicles ever to set wheel on rail – the *Schienenzeppelin*. This propeller driven contraption designed by Franz Kruckenberg was about as far removed from a practical passenger carrying train as you can get – although it did have a 40-seat saloon. Kruckenberg later developed a three-car diesel-hydraulic set which attained 215km/h on the eve of the second world war, setting a record for diesel traction

World record. Specially prepared TGV set 16 powered up to 380km/h near Moulins-en-Tonnerrois on France's Paris–Sud-Est line on 26 February 1981. *SNCF*

Collector's piece. A plaque commemorating the achievement of the world record speed for a passenger carrying train embellishes the side of a power car on TGV Set 16. *Author*

that was unbeaten until a Spanish train managed 222km/h in 1972. In the following year Britain's prototype High Speed Train beat this by 8km/h, but again a Spanish diesel came within less than 1km/h in 1978. BR only inched ahead once more in November 1986 during a test run for a new type of bogie (Chapter 15).

But even before the shortlived Kruckenberg wonder had established its niche in history, the Germans laid claim to the fastest absolute speed. Only 22 years after Werner von Siemens had pioneered the first electric train in Berlin in 1879, a four-axle electric locomotive developed by the Studiengesellschaft für Elektrische Schnellbahnen (Company for the Study of High Speed Electric Railways) crashed through the 160km/h barrier to hit a top speed of 162.5km/h on the 23km military railway between Marienfelde and Zossen south of Berlin. Powered by a 15kV supply at three-phase, this Siemens & Halske machine was followed by two six-axle railcars. They were substantial pieces of metal, and when one of them actually had a bogie lift off the track and spread it on landing the trials were called off until the permanent way had been rebuilt with heavier materials able to withstand the dynamic forces which have ever since been the bugbear of high speed running.

With heavier rail in place, the tests restarted, breaking through 200km/h to first 202.7, then a few days later to 206.8km/h. The climax came on 27 October 1903 when the AEG railcar motored up to 210.2km/h. But the complexity of three-phase power collection with each phase being fed on a separate wire at the side of the track demanded a veritable forest of side-contact pantographs on the traction units. This posed all manner of problems, and the system was not developed further for passenger-carrying operations.

The exploits near Berlin were very much the exception in that era, as practically all development was concentrated on the steam locomotive in all its wondrous forms. The earliest claims of 160km/h running date back to the 1890s when several US locomotives are said to have shattered the 100mph barrier. Lack of proof means that these claims must be treated circumspectly, as must that of a 193km/h peak in Great Britain with 4–6–0 Saint class locomotive *Lady of Lyons* in 1903.

Much ink has already flowed about whether the Great Western Railway's 4–4–0 *City of Truro* did or did not reach 102.3mph on Wellington bank on 9 May 1904, but it seems pretty certain that the highly respected train recorder Charles Rous-Marten failed to time the train accurately, although a speed of 100mph was quite likely. Another 30 years elapsed before a reliable record of a 100mph run with a steam locomotive was made in Britain when Sir Nigel Gresley's famous A1 (later A3) Pacific *Flying Scotsman* notched that speed on 30 November 1934 down the London & North Eastern Railway's Stoke Bank between Grantham and Peterborough.

The A1 was the first of a long line of Pacific power that kept the LNER in the forefront of high speed running as Gresley and his colleagues honed the development of the steam engine into a finely tuned breed of racehorses. It was the LNER that in September 1935 launched the streamlined age in Britain with a magnificent train built specially to run between London and Newcastle in a 4hr timing. This was the *Silver Jubilee*, motive power for which was another Gresley design, the A4 Pacific whose aerodynamic front end was a distinctive wedge shape that is still evoked by modern high speed hardware such as the TGV. On a demonstration run on 27 September the first A4, *Silver Link*, fresh from its birthplace at Doncaster, set up a British speed record of 181km/h.

Two more A4 hauled streamlined trains were commissioned on the East Coast route in 1937, by which time the West Coast route of the London Midland & Scottish Railway was reviving old rivalries for Anglo-Scottish traffic by launching its own streamliner, the *Coronation Scot* between London Euston and Glasgow which with Pacific haulage ran in a schedule that in the southbound direction was only 24min more than the average Glasgow–London electric timing of 1986.

On the press trip for this service the locomotive No 6220 *Coronation* thundered up to a speed of 181 or 183km/h (depending on whether you believe the timers on the train or the speed recorder on the locomotive) – but nearly at great cost, because the speed was reached on a downhill stretch just south of Crewe, and the brakes were only applied in the very nick of time to stop the whole convoy from being spreadeagled over Crewe station. It hit the reverse curves through the junctions south of the station at dangerous speed, sending nearly everyone aboard to the floor and spectacularly wrecking the crockery in the diner, but the train held to the track and stopped more or less at the platform.

It was on the East Coast, however, that the crowning achievement of the steam age was attained when A4 *Mallard* earned the distinction of the world's fastest steam locomotive with a magnificent dash at 126mph down Stoke Bank on 3 July 1938. This locomotive has been preserved and was returned to full working order in 1986.

The 1930s marked a zenith in steam locomotive development, particularly in the USA where some immensely powerful designs scorched the ground as they thundered across huge distances with enormous trains that dwarfed their European cousins. Some graceful beauties and some especially ugly monsters fought long and hard against the tyro diesels that were soon setting their own records. Sterling performances were turned in by the legendary K4s design of the Pennsylvania Railroad, while the Milwaukee Road attacked its rivals on the lucrative Chicago–Minneapolis–St Paul haul with some specially bred 4–4–2 and later much more powerful 4–6–4 locomotives that covered long sections of the 660km run at 160km/h with the famous *Hiawathas*.

But the diesels gained an unassailable foothold in 1934 when first the Burlington Railroad and then the Union Pacific smashed all previous transcontinental records with runs by the first two diesel streamliners, the *Pioneer Zephyr* and the M-10000, later put to work the *City of Salina* to and from Kansas City. On the first trip the *Pioneer Zephyr* attained 181km/h on 26 May 1934 on a run between Denver and Chicago. It was not long before bigger and more powerful diesels were displacing steam on the Burlington and the UP, and then elsewhere. This process continued through the 1930s and 1940s as the US railroads battled among themselves for clientele, while in the 1950s they were struggling to fight off the embryonic competition of the airlines.

Diesel traction progressed no less spectacularly in the country of its origin. The 1930s in Germany saw a succession of developments in high speed diesel traction which were far more significant than Kruckenberg's unique 18.5 tonne two-axle propeller-powered vehicle. During the 1920s the Reichsbahn had developed a series of railcars intended for branch line duties, and their design was extrapolated by Dr-Ing Fuchs and his colleague Oberrat Breuer of the Berlin central offices to produce a high speed articulated railcar with a pair of 410hp Maybach diesels driving electric motors powering the axles of the centre bogie. A test run on 19 December between Berlin and Hamburg confirmed the designer's predictions when the VT877 railcar set reached 165km/h. On 30 December a press trip brought fresh speed honours, and the railcar was immediately christened the *Fliegender Hamburger*.

On 15 May this train entered public service, covering the 287km between Berlin and Hamburg at an average of 124.7km/h, the maximum allowed being 160km/h. This was the naissance of a network of high speed diesel railcar services built up by the Reichsbahn to an amazing standard in the interval before war interrupted progress. The fastest speed achieved by one of these railcars – of which there were four principal types – was a peak of 205km/h with the Leipzig class early in 1936. By 1939 nearly all large German cities had a high speed railcar link to the capital, with several services running at *average* speeds of 120 to 130km/h over considerable distances.

The second world war brought another gap in the list of records and afterwards steam traction was clearly on the way out. The devastation of the war in Europe offered little chance for revival of the high speeds of the 1930s, and not until well into the 1950s were timings being restored to pre-war levels. There was spirited running with the big modern steam locomotives but slowly and surely they were giving way to electric and diesel traction. In the USA this period witnessed the collapse of the passenger business in the face of unbridled competition from the air and the highway.

The potential of electric traction was flung into focus by the spectacular drama of the 1955 speed trials in France, and these were followed by a long series of less dramatic but important tests that gave French railway engineers an essential insight into the problems of high speed running. This put French engineers in good stead as far as cutting regular inter-city journey times went – a much more daunting task than souping up one or two locomotives for a one-off record attempt under special conditions. The late 1950s saw the famous Paris–Marseilles–Nice *Mistral* claim the honours for Europe's fastest train, while other schedules to French provincial cities were gradually whittled down.

British Railways spearheaded an important advance in inter-city travel in Europe when amid some considerable controversy the Eastern, North Eastern and Scottish Regions invested in a diesel design that put all other main line diesels in Britain to shame. This was the superb 3,300hp Deltic, 22 of which entered service in 1961–62 after a prototype built by English Electric had demonstrated just what diesel traction was all about. The Deltics ushered in 100mph running on BR, and were an instant success. As time passed they were fine-tuned to match improvements to the track and the easing of curves on the East Coast route. Although they were followed by 100mph electrics on the West Coast route of the London Midland Region in 1966, the Deltic achievements were a turning point for inter-city rail travel in Britain.

At that time similar improvements were being made in Western Europe, with the famous *Rheingold* express of German Federal Railway being speeded up with some 160km/h running in 1962, but really high speed running, which is what the rest of this book is about, began somewhere else. The story switches to Japan.

# 2

# BULLET TRAINS REAP PROFITS

At the outer end of platforms 18 and 19 at Tokyo central station stands a small red brick monument. It commemorates Mr Shinji Sogo, the political father of the world's first dedicated high speed passenger railway. Japan's legendary blue and ivory bullet trains launched the adventure of 210km/h travel while Europe's railway engineers were still pondering a move from 160 to 200km/h.

On the crowded archipelago of Japan the idea of a high speed line along the southwest shore of the main island Honshu was first mooted in the 1930s. From the capital Tokyo the line was to run west to Osaka, then on to Shimonoseki at the western tip of the island looking across to Kyushu. High speed in those days was 125km/h, the fastest allowed on Japanese National Railways being a mere 100km/h. In 1939 plans had progressed to the point where the politicians were ready to approve the scheme. Some preliminary work was carried out in 1940, only to be halted immediately by the onset of war.

The old 1,067mm gauge Tokaido line had been completed in 1889, and JNR had electrified the route as far as Kyoto in 1956. But revival of Japan's economic fortunes after the second world war was turning the chain of cities along the corridor west of Tokyo into a booming industrial conurbation where demand for inter-city travel was rocketing. After electrification, JNR commissioned a study on how best to respond to the need to move many thousands of people a day between the burgeoning cities.

It was an obvious step to revive the pre-war idea of a high speed line, and the study published in 1957 built on the earlier proposal. Postulating a Tokyo–Osaka shinkansen (new trunk line), it suggested that the 515km trip could be accomplished in just three hours. The alternative would have been simply to finish quadrupling the existing route – some of it already had four or even six tracks – but in 1958 the

Ministry of Transport decided that a completely new line should be built instead. The government at once approached the World Bank to help fund construction.

It was Mr Shinji Sogo, JNR president, who steered the project through to completion. He was supported by the technical expertise of Mr Hideo Shima, then JNR's chief engineer. Shima led a team of far-sighted engineers who put together the technical matrix of ideas and hardware that gave the world its first high speed passenger railway.

Authorisation to build came at the end of 1958, and the first turf was cut in April 1959. Construction teams laboured flat out for just over five years, and the first trains ran in 1964 in time for that year's Olympic games in Tokyo.

The New Tokaido line was unique. Most importantly, it was built as a fully-integrated high speed package with special trains running on their own special track. Quite significant was the deliberate choice of a gauge not compatible with the rest of JNR's network. The 1,435mm gauge (4ft 8½in standard gauge) allowed a substantially higher speed than was possible on other JNR lines where the rails were only 1,067mm (3ft 6in) apart and sharp curves and level crossings proliferated. Equally important was the possibility of a wide body profile that would allow 2+3 seating. Yet another advantage was that no operating problems afflicting services on other JNR routes could spill over on to the premier line.

Originally, New Tokaido line trains were to have run at 260km/h, but the top speed was lowered to 210km/h halfway through the design phase on the strict insistence of the World Bank. Electrification was at 25kV 60Hz, the decision to use high voltage ac having been taken after successful trials at 20kV on the 29km Sendai–Sakunami section of the Senzan line on northern Honshu.

The shinkansen was also intended to carry freight in special containers, but this idea was soon dropped when it was found that daytime line capacity was at a premium for passenger trains and that the night hours had to be kept free for maintenance of track and overhead line equipment.

No level crossings were permissible. This is perhaps more significant in Japan than in many other countries – level crossings may interrupt busy commuter lines every 100 metres in the Tokyo suburbs. Hence about one third of the shinkansen route ran on bridges or viaducts.

Another 69km ran in tunnel. Steepest gradient was 2 per cent (1 in 50), but more usually 1.5 per cent; the sharpest curve had a radius of

2,500 metres. Track was of conventional design with 53g/m rail supported by concrete sleepers in a deep ballast bed.

JNR chose a multiple-unit formation for the shinkansen rolling stock. This had several advantages, such as rapid turnrounds at termini. It permitted the electrical equipment needed for the 8,900kW continuous power rating to be distributed along the length of the train, so ensuring that the weight was evenly spread and that axleloads did not exceed 16 tonnes. This was to avoid high dynamic forces being exerted on the track – a fundamental precept of high speed operations which other railways later found they could not ignore.

With a traction motor on each axle, a powerful rheostatic braking effort was available for use when braking from maximum speed. This was important as there were 10 intermediate stations between Tokyo and Osaka, requiring frequent brake applications. The electric brakes minimised wear and tear on the discs, which were only phased in at 50km/h.

Test running began on a short section in 1962 when a pair of prototype sets, one of two and one of four cars, was delivered from a consortium set up specially to build the New Tokaido line stock. Based at Kamonomiya in Kanagawa prefecture, the prototypes were put through a period of intense testing, culminating in a trip at 256km/h in March 1963. Orders were immediately placed for 360 cars, and many were delivered in time for the opening the following year.

In July 1964 a test train ran the whole way from Tokyo to Osaka on the new line, and limited service began on 25 August ahead of the official opening date of 1 October. Journey time was 4hr, representing an average speed of 128.7km/h. This compared with a 6½hr journey time on the old line.

Top speed was 210km/h, but this could not be exploited on much of the route because of numerous speed restrictions enforced where the track had not settled. In some cases the formation dropped significantly on embankments next to bridges, leading to 'hump-backed' river crossings.

The air-conditioned trains were formed of 12 cars in six electrical pairs, each pair having its own pantograph. The pantograph car carried the transformer and rectifier, its neighbour housing control apparatus and the braking resistors.

Inside, the seating layout was unique to each pair. Two cars had buffet counters and two offered 2+2 seating as green cars (the Japanese equivalent of first class); the rest of the cars had 2+3 seating. The streamlined nose with a prominent dome illuminated at night engendered the bullet appellation.

Bullet train beauty. The classic shot of a bullet train speeding past Mount Fuji on Japan's Tokaido shinkansen line helped to publicise the debut of the world's first start-to-stop schedules exceeding 160km/h in 1965.

As there was only one type of train, braking characteristics were the same for all services, so that signalling and other equipment did not have to take into account different braking distances or operating speeds. There are no lineside signals and speed instructions are transmitted to the driver by pulse-modulated audio-frequency track circuits. A receiver on the leading car detects the pulse frequency, and the corresponding speed is displayed on a panel in front of the driver. Although JNR canvassed the possibility of automatic driving, it opted to leave the driver with his traditional role, although if he exceeds the maximum line speed indicated on his cab instruments the brakes are automatically applied.

JNR chose a service pattern with two types of train: *Hikari* (light) which called only at Nagoya and Kyoto, and *Kodama* (echo) which stopped at all the intermediate stations. To begin with 30 trains a day were scheduled in each direction. In the first few weeks of operation every day saw 60,000 passengers ride the shinkansen, but the daily total rapidly increased, and a staggering 11 million had been carried within three months. Before long, the line began to turn in a profit.

## Global première

In October 1965, with the track firmly bedded in, JNR speeded up services to give a Tokyo–Osaka time of 3hr 10min. Average speed was 162.6km/h, easily the fastest scheduled passenger service in the world. It was truly a global première, as no train service anywhere had ever before exceeded a start-to-stop average of 100mph.

Although the original 3hr target had not been attained, mainly because the Kyoto stop was not envisaged, the bullet trains were fast enough to attract unprecedented levels of business, and by 1966 the number of passengers a day had doubled. By this time JNR was running 44 trains a day in each direction, and only a short interval elapsed before there were 51.

To travel on the world's fastest trains passengers had to pay a hefty supplement on top of the express fare, but speed was what the population wanted. They flocked to the new service, and the profit mushroomed. This fact did not escape the attention of visionary railway engineers in Europe who were keeping a close watch on developments in Japan.

Revenue was outpacing all costs, including interest payments on the original capital. Japan lies in a zone of tectonic activity, and JNR was conscious of the dangers that earthquakes posed to its new golden goose. In 1966 seismometers were installed along the track to detect earthquakes – if the tremor reached a pre-set level, it triggered equipment that automatically halted the trains.

On 13 July 1967 JNR celebrated its 100 millionth shinkansen passenger. The government and JNR were greatly encouraged, and in 1967 work began on an extension from Shin Osaka to Okayama.

Meanwhile JNR decided to expand its overstretched fleet of shinkansen cars by lengthening trains from 12 to 16 cars. A 16-car train was tested in June 1968 and all *Hikari* trains were lengthened to 16 cars in February 1970 in time for opening of the Expo 70 world exposition in Osaka the following month.

A new station was opened at Mishima, about 40km southeast of the 3,776 metre high peak of Mount Fuji in April 1969, and traffic continued to boom. In the same year 5 May saw more than half a million passengers carried in a single day.

Shinkansen traffic soared from strength to strength, and the airlines watched helplessly as passengers deserted planes for trains. Short-haul air schedules along the western Honshu corridor were pared back, but for the moment the long-haul routes to Okayama, Hiroshima and to western Honshu were immune. The extension to Okayama was worrying airline executives, however.

The 164km extension was called the New Sanyo line, Sanyo being that part of Honshu that looks towards Japan's Inland Sea. Experience of 2½ years running on the New Tokaido line had taught JNR that higher standards would be needed if the goal of 260km/h was to be attained, so more generous track parameters were chosen. The minimum curve radius was enlarged to 4,000 metres and the distance between track centres increased from 4.2 to 4.3 metres.

Altogether 94km of route ran on viaduct or bridges with 57km in tunnel, the 16km Rokko tunnel being the longest. Intermediate stations were built at Shin Kobe, Nishi Akashi, Himeji and Aioi. Shin Kobe station is sandwiched tightly between two tunnels, neatly illustrating the difficulties of building new railways in Japan. Here the strip of land between the mountains and the sea is so cramped that the city of Kobe is expanding into the sea on huge artificial islands!

Still the Tokaido line pulled in business. Profits were turned in year after year, a fact which undoubtedly influenced the Ministry of Transport's decision for JNR to proceed with a second extension in 1969. This formed a 398km continuation of the Sanyo line with nine intermediate stations from Okayama to Hakata; work began in 1970. Biggest single task was construction of the 18.7km Shin Kammon tunnel under the narrow strait between Honshu and Kyushu; it was completed in the space of four years.

Constructed to the same high standards as the Okayama extension, the second part of the Sanyo line ran along a narrow coastal belt beyond Fukuyama or cut inland through the mountains. Construction on the first part between Shin Osaka and Okayama had been somewhat easier, but so little land was available beyond Okayama that well over half of the route to Hakata had to be in tunnel. Nearly a third was on bridges or viaducts.

One of the lessons learnt from the Tokaido line was that the steel girder bridges constructed in heavily built-up areas were a source of unacceptable noise and vibration; this had led to vociferous protests by lineside residents. So on the extensions JNR substituted concrete for steel. In a bid to reduce maintenance costs concrete slab track replaced conventional ballast and sleepers.

To begin with the New Tokaido line had automatic route setting at certain intermediate stations: *Kodama* trains routed themselves into side platforms if they were to be overtaken by a following *Hikari*. Only when trains were running late or out of sequence did dispatchers have to intervene. At other stations dispatchers set the routes, but as traffic grew their task became impracticable. So JNR introduced a computerised traffic control system called Comtrac in 1972. This relieved the dispatchers of routine operations and proposed revised schedules when services were disrupted.

On the day that Comtrac was commissioned, JNR opened the extension to Okayama; it was 15 March 1972. Before that there were 78 *Hikari* and 134 *Kodama* services a day. The pattern of service included three types of *Hikari*: one taking 4hr 10min from Tokyo to Okayama and running non-stop on the new line, one with two intermediate stops and one with four. *Kodama* trains continued to call at all stations. The service was a phenomenal success, and records for the number of passengers carried in a day were set regularly. Over 640,000 people rode the shinkansen on 6 May 1973.

In 1969 the Japanese cabinet approved the New Comprehensive National Development Plan. The document included plans for construction of 7,200km of shinkansen – a real nationwide network. The whole lot was to be completed by 1985.

In May 1970 the Diet (Japanese parliament) passed a remarkable piece of legislation: the Law for the Construction of Nationwide High Speed Railways. This set the scene by stating that a high speed transport system would play an important role in the comprehensive and extensive development of the nation, going on to describe the objective of the law as 'to construct a nationwide high-speed railway network to promote the growth of the national economy and enlarge people's sphere of activity.'

Five lines were allocated priority:

- Tohoku line; Tokyo to Sapporo on Hokkaido
- Joetsu line; Tokyo to Niigata on the Sea of Japan coast
- Hokuriku line; Tokyo to Osaka via Toyama on the Sea of Japan
- Kyushu line from Hakata to Kagoshima with a branch to Nagasaki
- Tokyo to the city's new international airport at Narita.

In April 1971 the Ministry of Transport issued a directive for the Japan Railway Construction Corporation to start work on the New Tohoku line and the New Joetsu line. Cost of the route to Hokkaido was put at ¥835 billion and price tag for the much shorter but more difficult route to Niigata was ¥580 billion or ¥2.1 billion per km.

By this time JNR was encountering serious opposition to further high speed line construction. The main problem was noise and vibration suffered by lineside residents whose dwellings in some cases almost touched the viaduct structures. There had been little opposition at the outset as there had been fewer trains. As the number of services grew, so did levels of noise and vibration.

In the worst cases the only solution seemed to be to rehouse people further away from the line. The problem was taken up by the Environment Agency which submitted recommendations to the Ministry of Transport in December 1972. Shinkansen noise in residential areas was not to exceed 80dBA, and where it was more than 85dBA special sound protection measures were to be taken. For JNR the cost of meeting these stringent standards was huge; 1.9 metre high lineside walls had to be erected. But worse was to come.

While JNR struggled to hush the noise, it was suddenly confronted with a new problem. Almost overnight the world was thrown into confusion as the oil crisis erupted in 1973–74. Japan, with no oil of its own, was particularly vulnerable. Railways had at first predicted the oil crisis to be their salvation, and it certainly did persuade governments, notably in France, to look sympathetically at electrification schemes. But it was not a panacea. The immediate effect was to send the world's economy reeling on a downward spiral, with railways suffering as much as any other industry.

In Japan, public spending had to be reined in, and although rail transport based on energy consumption figures alone was the most efficient mode, the high cost of shinkansen construction militated against the rapid expansion outlined in the Law for Construction of Nationwide High Speed Railways.

In the meantime construction teams pressed on with the Sanyo extension. On 10 March 1975 JNR President Matsutaro Fujii rode the first *Hikari* from Hakata to Tokyo at 06.06, passing en route a *Kodama* that had been sent off from Okayama by Transport Minister Matsuo Kimura. But the storm clouds were gathering, and on the very day that trains began running to Hakata hurricane strength winds and a power failure delayed nearly half a million shinkansen passengers. It was a bad omen.

A few days later the Central Council for Environmental Pollution published even stricter noise levels that JNR engineers dismissed as impractical without resorting to drastic measures such as buying up huge swathes of lineside property. While the new limits were practically impossible to achieve on the existing routes, it was obvious that future lines would have to comply with them.

This was one reason why JNR's President Fujii announced on 28 January 1975 that opening of the Tohoku shinkansen was to be delayed from 1977 until 1979. Already the cost had risen to ¥1,500,000 million. At one stage work actually ground to a halt. The original dream of 260km/h running with which Mr Sogo and Mr Shima had set out seemed further away than ever. Top speed was still 210km/h on the Sanyo line, but much lower limits applied at the southern extremity of the route, bringing the Tokyo–Hakata average speed down significantly.

It was not only the two northern routes that were behind schedule. The shinkansen to Tokyo's new international airport 65km away from the city centre at Narita was also the subject of dispute. The airport itself had aroused bitter and at times violent opposition from local residents, and the prospect of high speed trains – now equated with noise – on top of the roar of hundreds of jumbo jets merely added fuel to the fire.

Work on the Narita shinkansen had begun in 1974, and a shell for a new station was finished under the airport terminals. But construction ceased prematurely when local residents made their feelings evident in no uncertain terms. Faced with the outcry, the government told JNR to see if conventional trains could be run to Narita instead.

When Narita airport finally opened in 1978, rail service was not provided by JNR, but by the Keisei Electric Railway. Some five years earlier Keisei had built a short branch into the airport at its own expense. It had also purchased some *Skyliner* trains to work the line, but they had languished in mothballs for the first few years of their life while disputes raged round the runways. With the airport open, Keisei's decisions were vindicated at last. Meanwhile, weeds sprouted on the alignment of the Narita shinkansen.

# 3
# EARLY DAYS IN THE 200 CLUB

Japan's bold venture into the high speed era with trains running day-in day-out at 210km/h was a stunning achievement. More than a decade elapsed before any other railway was able even remotely to emulate it.

The tentative steps of the European railways to join the 200km/h club were timid by comparison, while in North America there was a failure to understand the fundamentals of high speed trains.

European conditions are markedly different from those in Japan, with no single corridor having the same density of population as the remarkable human antheap between Tokyo and Osaka. To begin with at least the Europeans saw little justification for engineering a dedicated high speed line from scratch, so they set out to raise inter-city speeds on their old lines – most of which dated from the 19th century. This approach was dramatically cheaper, but it was beset with problems which the Japanese had not encountered.

The German Federal Railway (DB) was first to the starting post for 200km/h, initially for a series of isolated sprints that were a far cry from the all-day marathon between Tokyo and cities west. Nonetheless, high speed news hogged the German headlines only a few months after the Japanese bullet trains.

An international transport exhibition was staged in Munich in 1965, and DB saw this as an opportunity to publicise its prestige expresses, by then achieving quite creditable average speeds over long distances on a network that had been badly ravaged by the second world war. On 26 June 1965, the first day of the exhibition, hundreds of schoolchildren carrying balloons and flags turned out to watch a seven-car special depart for Augsburg, some 60km to the northwest.

At the head was a locomotive that had been delivered only four months earlier – prototype Co-Co electric No E03 001. Finished in red and cream livery, this impressive machine packed an hourly rating of 6,420kW, with a 10min output of 9,000kW (12,000hp) – enough to accelerate an eight coach train up to 200km/h in 3min.

The special was flagged away at 10.00 precisely by Bavarian State Premier Dr Goppel, and the E03 eased it out of the temporary exhibition station to join the main line at Pasing. Hostesses had been detailed to give technical particulars to the guests, but everyone's attention was rivetted on the speedometers specially mounted in the cars. Speed rose steadily as the train headed north until spontaneous applause broke out as the needles settled briefly on 205km/h. Only 26min after departure the train drew into the platforms at Augsburg.

Using E03 001 and its three sisters, DB repeated the performance for the public every day until 3 October. For the paltry sum of DM4 exhibition visitors could buy a ticket for the 200km/h special that left the exhibition grounds daily at 13.20. The 200km/h ceiling was only permitted northbound between Lochhausen and Olching (4km), and from Malching to Kissing (26.5km); southbound a 26.7km stretch from Mehring to Gernlinden and a 1.4km section near Lochhausen were available.

A second round trip (and on some days a third) was staged at weekends leaving Munich at 16.33, but because of traffic density on the main line this was limited to 160km/h – tickets were priced down to DM3 to compensate.

During the exhibition no less than 222 high speed trips were made, but they were essentially publicity stunts. Although DB was strictly correct in describing them as regularly-timetabled trains, they were really rather a flash in the pan. It was the same on 11 and 17 November 1965 when specials were run at 200km/h for an international conference in Munich. Considerable time and investment was needed to fettle up DB's routes for regular running at this speed.

Back in 1962 DB had upped the speed of its prestige *Rheingold* express to 160km/h, and in the following year tests at 200km/h began on the 25km line between Forchheim and Bamberg. The problem with 200km/h was how to stop – it was not possible in the standard DB braking distance. So special arrangements had to be made for the driver to 'see' beyond the next signal. An inductive cable in the track was used to transmit information about signal aspects and speed restrictions to the train; on board the locomotive a computer calculated the maximum speed at which the train could run and still halt before the next stop signal.

This 'target' speed was displayed in the driver's cab together with the actual speed. If actual speed exceeded the target speed, the brakes were applied automatically. Called *Linienzugbeinflussung* (LZB) this

Shortlived hopes. German Federal Railway's Hamburg–Munich Trans-Europ-Express *Blauer Enzian* first ran at 200km/h in 1968, but in the following year the maximum was pruned back to 160km/h. Hauled by one of four prototype Class E03 locos, the train is seen here at Möhren between Donauwörth and Treuchtlingen. *Ralf Roman Rossberg*

system complemented the conventional signals and safety equipment; it was to become mandatory for 200km/h operations in West Germany.

DB launched its first regular timetabled services at 180km/h on 28 May 1967, but Munich–Augsburg was the only line cleared for the new maximum. DB wanted to plunge straight into 200km/h after the 1965 exhibition, but the Ministry of Transport had ruled against this because there were still level crossings on the route. With these out of the way, 1968 saw the ceiling lifted to 200km/h.

Only one train was involved – the Hamburg–Munich Trans-Europ-Express *Blauer Enzian*. With five intermediate stops on the 813km haul, average speed was only 106km/h. But DB's foray into the realm of 200km/h was shortlived. Because of alterations to the LZB (and excessive wear and tear on the track), the ceiling was pruned back to 160km/h in 1969, and the *Blauer Enzian* decelerated.

## France joins the club

In 1967 the French made a more successful bid to join the 200km/h club and stay there. Influenced by the success of the bullet trains and with a wealth of experience accumulated during a long programme of high speed trials in France, senior SNCF officials had decided in 1964–65 that 200km/h would be introduced in 1967 over a section of the Paris–Toulouse line, electrified at 1.5kV dc. The train chosen for the launch was the prestige *Capitole* which offered a first class only business service to the home of the French aircraft industry, Toulouse.

SNCF's management counted among it an audacious team of men prepared to stake their future on their expertise. André Prud'Homme was well respected as a permanent way expert, while the doyen of the traction engineers Fernand Nouvion was revered for his pioneering work in the development of 25kV during the 1950s; Nouvion had also been the driving force behind the 1955 trials. Had these men opposed the 200km/h launch, it would undoubtedly have been stillborn. As it was there was considerable trepidation, for SNCF engineers could not erase the memory of the sudden onset of bogie instability which had nearly wreaked catastrophe in 1955.

Like the Germans, the French opted for a locomotive plus coaches formation for the high speed debut. A fleet of 22 coaches was allocated for the two sets needed for the service – the standard 350 tonne formation was six compartment cars, one of which had van space, and a diner of the latest type; two extra cars could be added without affecting the timings. The spare cars were frequently used, particularly on Friday evenings when two complete trains were run from Paris. Apart from the diners, the cars conformed to a standard UIC design with no air-conditioning; they were distinguished from other stock by electromagnetic rail brakes which permitted the emergency braking distance to be cut from 2,200 metres at 200km/h to 1,600 metres.

As with the *Blauer Enzian*, the *Capitole* was allocated a fleet of four locomotives. These were Type BB9200 four-axle machines with a relatively modest continuous power rating of around 4,000kW; two of them had previously been used for trials at up to 250km/h. Modifications for hauling the *Capitole* included changes to the gear ratios, installation of a preselection speed control system and fitting of tough 23mm thick windscreens to protect the crews. Maroon livery with a grey band matched the coaches.

A track-circuit based cab signalling system indicating to the driver the maximum speed permissible in accordance with traffic and line conditions ahead was installed on the 200km/h section between Les Aubrais and Vierzon. This overcame the problem of the driver not having enough time to observe and react to lineside signals at the higher speed. Practically nothing was done to the already high quality track which nonetheless included sections of 18 metre jointed rails on wooden sleepers.

When the time came for the launch on 28 May 1967, SNCF had assembled a whole package of measures that cut 40min off the 713km run between Paris and Toulouse. Shorter station stops at Limoges and other towns helped to win a few minutes. Speed limits had been lifted on numerous sections, with the *Capitole* being permitted to run through curves at higher speeds than other trains. Over the 46km between Guillerval (66km out from Paris) and Cercottes just before Les Aubrais, it had clearance to cruise at 170km/h. The result was an end-to-end timing of 6hr, giving an average speed of 119km/h; over the 400km from Paris to Limoges the average was a laudable 138km/h. Interestingly enough, the short sprint at 200km/h contributed fewer minutes to the net time saving than the other refinements.

SNCF's clientele took the higher curving speeds in good part, soon getting to know when they had to hang on to their glasses and bottles in the diner. The fears about bogie instability at 200km/h proved unfounded; nor did the wheels have to be turned as often as envisaged.

Meantime, all was not well across the Rhine. An unlucky spate of four accidents within five months in 1971 stirred up controversy over DB's ambition to restore 200km/h running. Massively adverse press coverage out of all proportion to the events did nothing to bolster DB's shaken confidence, resulting in a decision to maintain the maximum speed of its recently introduced two-hourly Intercity services at 160km/h.

Apart from a few runs with the ET403 electric multiple-units in the early 1970s, DB did not reintroduce 200km/h in commercial service until May 1977. Even then, it was slipped in with no publicity and drivers had instructions only to run at 200km/h to regain lost time. Another year went by before it was permitted regularly, not just on the Munich–Augsburg line but also on the next section north from Augsburg to Donauwörth. In the flat plains of north Germany two other routes were cleared for the new maximum: Hamburg–Bremen and Uelzen–Hanover.

## North American tribulations

The USA was the only other country which made a serious application to join the 200km/h club in the 1960s. After pioneering some of the earliest diesel flyers in the 1930s the US railroads were among the world leaders in luxury high speed trains. That all changed after the second world war. The arrival of jet airliners and superhighways forced many railroads to liquidate their passenger trains. Huge distances favoured the jets, and only in the northeast were cities close enough for inter-city trains to compete with the Boeings.

It was in the days of the Pennsylvania Railroad in the mid-1960s that the feasibility of high-performance trains running at 258km/h (160mph) was first mooted. The 1965 High Speed Ground Transportation Act was followed less than a year later by agreement for a high speed demonstration service to run on the electrified Northeast Corridor route between New York and the federal capital. The idea was to cut journey time for the 364km run to just 2hr, although slower schedules with new trains were to begin on 29 October 1967, a remarkably ambitious target. A second demonstration service was to run over the 370km north from New York to Boston.

Before the demonstration projects could be translated from paper to hardware other circumstances conspired to twist the course of events. On 1 February 1968 the Pennsylvania merged with the New York Central to form the biggest US railroad company, Penn Central, which proceeded to file for bankruptcy just over two years later. This spectacular collapse did nothing to encourage government support for railroads, least of all for those that still carried passengers.

But Penn Central had been strengthening its 11kV 25Hz catenary, laying welded track and renewing sleepers and ballast in readiness for the start of its high speed demonstrations, designed to prove that passenger trains did have a future. The railroad was paying about four fifths of the cost, the other fifth coming from government coffers by courtesy of the Department of Transportation.

As the 1960s gave way to the 1970s the idea of a government subsidised corporation for passenger trains took root, and after a lot of legal brouhaha, Amtrak, officially the National Railroad Passenger Corporation, came into being on 1 May 1971.

Amtrak inherited the Penn Central's legacy of the demonstration projects, for which new trains had been ordered back in the 1960s. For the Washington–New York run 50 sophisticated *Metroliner* cars, each with four hefty dc traction motors with a 224kW continuous power rating, had been contracted from the famous Budd Co at a price of $21.6 million. In the same year Budd outshopped four test cars based on the successful *Silverliners* of the early 1960s to serve as mobile laboratories and prototypes for the demo trains. They ran trials over the first segment of the Corridor to be prepared for high speed running, the 35km between Trenton and New Brunswick, New Jersey. An apogée was attained on 24 May 1967 when the test train, packed with mediamen and railroad executives, was worked up to 251km/h.

But before Budd and its subcontractors were able to digest the lessons of the *Silverliner* trials, let alone translate them into viable hardware for the *Metroliners*, the politicians were demanding to see the results of their investment in high speed passenger railways. So it was that production of the *Metroliners*, being built in three versions – saloon, snack-bar and parlour cars – was pushed through with almost indecent haste.

1967 also saw a scheme emerge to institute high speed passenger service along the Philadelphia–Harrisburg–Pittsburgh axis. A Pennsylvania High Speed Ground Transportation Authority was to be set up; although this idea never matured properly, 11 identical *Metroliner* cars were added to the Budd order by the Southeastern Pennsylvania Transportation Authority to operate over the 166km between Philadelphia and Harrisburg.

By the time the October 1967 start-up date arrived the first seven *Metroliners* had only just left Budd's Philadelphia works. During early trials a set of the new cigar-shaped stainless steel cars managed to clock 264km/h, but this belied the headaches afflicting the commissioning teams. A Senate committee was appointed to examine the problems in June 1968, whereupon it emerged that no *Metroliner* was likely to carry passengers until the following year.

The *Metroliners* represented an attempt by the Americans to build their own bullet train without incurring bullet train costs, but the result was far from satisfactory. Experience in high speed train operation had evaporated after the war, and attempts to introduce all manner of sophisticated lightweight trains in the 1950s had met with varying degrees of disaster. The *Metroliners* had a pretty demanding design specification – they had to be able to accelerate to 193km/h in 2min, reaching 241km/h, 16km/h short of their maximum, in a further 60sec. Partly because of their own shortcomings, but more especially because the busy Northeast Corridor with its mix of slow heavy freights, scurrying commuter trains and frequent inter-city services was simply not suitable for sustained high speed running without major surgery, the *Metroliners* never made it into the 200 club.

The high 18.7 tonne axleload (16 tonnes on the shinkansen) with a considerable amount of unsprung weight was one explanation for the rough riding, which together with power equipment faults swiftly conferred on the *Metroliners* an unenviable reputation. Other problems included thermal stress in the wheels during braking, current collection difficulties, and bugs in the electronics. The Southeastern Pennsylvania Transportation Authority rejected its 11 cars, which were in due course added to the Northeast Corridor fleet.

Protracted rows followed between the builders and operators, and it was not until 16 January 1969 that the first *Metroliner* carried its first fare-paying passengers. As more cars trickled into service, the number of *Metroliner* schedules was stepped up, and on 2 April a non-stop 2hr 30min run averaging just over 144km/h was introduced.

Six days later the first of a new breed of trains began service on the New York–Boston leg of the Corridor. This was a three-car version of five seven-car gas turbine trainsets that the United Aircraft Corporation had leased to Canadian National for its Montreal–Toronto run, where they were expected to operate at 193km/h, UAC had conceived the Canadian version of the trains for 200km/h, but it was not to be.

First, the Canadian authorities set a ceiling of 153km/h on account of the number of level crossings, and second, the trains were little short of a technical catastrophe, although they also suffered from a good deal of bad luck. Incidentally, the level crossing hazard was proved real enough when one of the sets smashed into a lorryload of frozen meat during a press run on 10 December 1968. The glass fibre nose of the leading dome power car was crushed, but the structure was sufficiently undamaged for the same train to inaugurate passenger service two days later.

The UAC turbos had their origins in research on lightweight designs and single axle running gear carried out a few years earlier by the Chesapeake & Ohio. Power was supplied from four turbines in each end car driving both axles in the leading bogie through a common gearbox; in the case of the two US sets a dc traction motor was incorporated to permit the trains to run on third rail supply into New York's Grand Central terminus. The aerodynamically designed cars were all of light alloy construction, which gave a loaded weight of around 223 tonnes for the Canadian version. An extraordinary single-axle articulation was developed to join the cars. It incorporated pendular suspension (of which more in the next chapter) and a turnbuckle arrangement to ensure the axles stayed at right angles to the track. The end power bogies were if anything even more complex.

Despite the manufacturers' claims to the contrary, the ride was poor and the suspension system gave endless trouble. During the early years of their life, the Canadian sets seemed to spend more time out of service than in. Extensive modifications were made, much to UAC's chagrin. Somewhat ironically the three-car US sets, which were designed for 257km/h running as part of the New York–Boston demonstration project, performed rather better than their cousins north of the border. The first US train was powered up to 274.9km/h on 20 December 1967, but when it entered revenue service in 1969 the old bugs reappeared, forcing it to be taken out of use on the following two days.

Admittedly, the old New Haven track on the New York–Boston run militated against the turbos turning in fast timings. They did allow schedules to be cut to 3hr 39min, but it was a rather pathetic average of 109km/h; the best performance was a trial run completed in 3hr 4min, including four stops. The US turbos remained in service long enough for passengers to get to like them, but Amtrak, which was all too conscious of the turbines' thirst for fuel, eventually stored them out of use.

The Canadian trains suffered a worse fate. The Montreal–Toronto turbo service had to be suspended four times because of technical failures, and the sets were eventually reformed into three nine-car units. A fire on 29 May 1979 destroyed several cars, prompting Via Rail Canada, the Canadian equivalent of Amtrak, to take them out of service again. The cars that escaped the fire staggered back into service until 1982, when Via finally withdrew them for good. Their remains were offered for sale in the following year.

The turbos had a successor called the LRC (Light Rapid Comfortable or Léger Rapide Confortable). This was a joint venture by a group of Canadian companies keen to get aboard the high speed bandwagon that was so obviously rolling in the wake of the bullet trains.

The first light alloy bodied LRC car was demonstrated in Ottawa in October 1971 after a four-year gestation period. Unlike the UAC turbos, the LRC was based on proven techniques – apart from the servo-operated hydraulic body tilting mechanism. A conventional diesel locomotive with a low body and streamlined profile matching the coaches provided motive power, and a prototype unit joined the coach in 1972.

Both locomotive and coach had been built speculatively by the promoters, and they were put through a test programme that embraced a seven week séjour at the US Transportation Test Center in Pueblo, Colorado, during 1974. While there, they completed a 1,760km trip round the endurance loop at an average speed of 159km/h. The same duo established a Canadian speed record of 208km/h two years later.

Persistence by the promoters paid off, and in 1977 Amtrak agreed to lease two LRC sets. In November of that year the Canadian government further rewarded the suppliers' patience with an order for 22 power cars rated at 3,700hp and 50 coaches – enough to form 10 push-pull sets with two spare traction units.

The first of these was delivered to Via Rail Canada in 1981. Via planned to slash inter-city timings in its Quebec–Windsor corridor. Exploiting the LRC's 200km/h maximum speed on upgraded track would, Via fondly hoped, permit a Montreal–Ottawa timing of 1hr compared with the 1981 fastest time of 2hr 20min. By renewing more track between Ottawa and Toronto a 3hr 40min timing for the Montreal–Ottawa–Toronto run seemed feasible.

These hopes have never been realised. A strike at the Bombardier locomotive works in Montreal badly held up deliveries of the power cars, and when the trains were finally assembled all manner of irritating teething troubles prevented them from entering service. A few unadvertised trips were made in the autumn of 1981, but January 1982 saw LRC service suspended indefinitely while they were modified. They did go to work in March, and Via shortly afterwards announced that it was to buy 10 more LRC sets – but the announcement coincided with the return of the two six-car LRCs on loan to Amtrak which had used them on the turbos' old stamping ground be-

Light, Rapid, Comfortable. The LRC power car with its 25 tonne axleload is anything but light and the train is certainly not rapid by world standards. This is one of two LRC sets which Amtrak leased in 1981 working the *Beacon Hill* between New Haven and Boston.

Russian riddle. The ER200 was shown to the world at an exhibition in 1977, but only in the mid-1980s did it enter service between Moscow and Leningrad at its design speed of 200km/h. It runs once a week in each direction; a second round trip was to be added in January 1988.

tween New York and Boston since October 1981.

Only in June 1982 did the LRCs officially take up their duties – in timings which in some cases were inferior to those which the ill-fated turbos had clocked in the 1970s. For a time Canadian National forbade the LRCs to exceed 129km/h, intimating that the tilting was responsible for the track being spread. Their maximum speed was later fixed at 153km/h, but the tilt mechanism was not exploited. The 25 tonne axleload of the power car certainly militated against high speed operation – it went against the cardinal principle of low axleloads and low unsprung mass.

By 1983 LRCs had cut the 265.4km run from Montreal to Quebec to 2hr 30min, while one set pared the 444.6km between Ottawa and Toronto to less than 5hr. But the early ambitions had been thwarted, and Via had a struggle to keep the LRCs in traffic – there have been occasions when availability has plunged well below 50 per cent. The LRC's future as a high speed train can safely be discounted.

Back in the Northeast Corridor in 1969 the *Metroliners* had begun to show promise. Patronage grew surprisingly fast, with load factors of around 80 per cent in the first few months of public service. While the original targets remained out of reach, progress was sufficiently good to attract a loyal and steadily growing clientele. After two years' service the trains had carried over 2 million passengers.

But the troubles were not over. Excessive maintenance costs and high downtime prompted a reappraisal, and in 1973 a quartet of cars was extensively rebuilt. The price proved to be astronomical, and Amtrak cast around for a more cost-effective successor.

The American essay to join Japan and France in the 200km/h club was followed by a host of other attempts as railway managements around the world sought the kudos and the commercial advantages that high speeds offered. Perhaps most surprising of all was the Soviet Union's bid to score a high speed success.

On the face of it, the Soviet railways are quite unsuited to high speed operation, their main job being to shift vast quantities of freight – more than all the US railroads handle together. The world's largest single railway is efficient in the same sense as a carthorse, with endless successions of slow moving wagons interspersed by long rakes of passenger coaches trundling at similar speeds.

On the famous Moscow–Leningrad line of the October Railway, however, things were different. The 650km route electrified at 3kV dc is almost entirely straight, and for many years a summer-only working of the crack *Aurora* had been timed to complete the trip in 4hr 59min in one direction only.

In 1971 details were revealed of a 14 car trainset intended to offer a 4hr timing between Leningrad and the Soviet capital at speeds up to 200km/h. Built by Riga Carriage Works, the ER200 broke the mould of Soviet coach design with bodies constructed of aluminium alloy. By 1975 a six-car version had been worked up to 206km/h on a test track at the Shcherbinka research institute near Moscow, and a four-car version ran joy rides for visitors to an exhibition staged at the institute in 1977.

The ER200 was matched against a rival called the *Russian Troika* which consisted of a rake of lightweight coaches assembled at the Kalinin works and hauled by a mammoth eight-axle twin-unit ChS200 locomotive. Two of these 150 tonne giants with an 8,000kW power rating were built as prototypes by Skoda in Czechoslovakia. In 1979 Soviet Railways took delivery of a batch of 20, half of which were geared to run at 200km/h, but none are operating at their maximum speed.

The 200km/h target was to prove even more elusive than it had for the other superpower. Neither the *Troika* nor the ER200 met the demands of the Soviet track engineers who were concerned about damage inflicted at high speed stemming from too much unsprung mass on the axles – even though axleload on the ER200 was just 16.1 tonnes. Numerous announcements were made about the ER200 entering service, but time and time again the event was postponed until credibility was severely damaged.

Only in March 1984 did the ER200 carry its first fare-paying passengers. Despite being allowed to cruise at 180km/h, it was booked to run in the old *Aurora* schedule of 4hr 59min. It ran on Thursdays only from Leningrad to Moscow, returning on the Friday. By 1986 the speed maximum had been raised to 200km/h and the schedule cut to 4hr 39min, but it still had only a weekly sortie.

High speed plans were again dusted off in the summer of 1987, when Soviet Railways ordered 10 R-200 trainsets based on the ER200 design to work Moscow – Leningrad services from 1991. Meanwhile from January 1988 two weekly round trips were expected to be worked by ER200 formations.

More ambitious is the plan for a high speed line from Moscow to the Black Sea, needed apparently to ease congestion on prime Holiday routes. Dubbed Moscow – South, the idea first surfaced in 1980, and in 1987 the Ministry of Transport set a team of 300 engineers to work on preliminary designs for a 1,700km route to Simferepol with speed maxima ranging from 250 to 350km/h. They are due to submit a report on the 5 billion rouble mega-project by October 1988.

# 4

# FROM THE BULLET TO THE BASCULANTE

Whereas North America charged precipitately into the high speed age, with fairly disastrous results, the tremors generated by the shinkansen caused a more sedate reaction across the Atlantic. By the late 1960s, however, a caucus of high speed train proposals was starting to gel. In most cases these were not special sets of cars souped-up for 200km/h, but prototypes of supertrains aimed at even higher speeds. Some eight years elapsed before the first of these shinkansen clones appeared in Europe.

In 1972 five sets of different high speed hardware took to the rails in Western Europe. Four had as a common feature a form of body-tilting designed to allow them to run through curves up to 40 per cent faster than conventional trains. Cornering faster was a prime means of saving time on sinuous lines, and how to achieve it had exercised the minds of high speed engineers for a number of years.

When a train speeds through a curve, passengers tend to be thrown towards the outside of the curve by centrifugal force. To counteract this effect the outer rail is positioned higher than the inner rail, creating a cant. Where the speed is higher than that at which the cant negates the centrifugal force, a cant deficiency arises. On most routes the angle of cant is limited because otherwise the inner rail would be overloaded – the angle of cant must also allow for the possibility of a train being stationary on the curve. The problem is exacerbated by soft secondary suspension on some types of modern coach, causing the bodies to lean outwards by as much as 2°.

The difficulty had not arisen on the shinkansen because there was no curve of a radius smaller than 2,500 metres (apart from on the approaches to Tokyo where the line follows the alignment of other JNR lines); nor did it apply particularly on the largely straight Munich–Augsburg line. The French in 1967 had opted simply to subject *Capitole* passengers to the higher forces and put up with any complaints, but other railways believed this unacceptable. In any case, they were contemplating going beyond 200km/h.

So emerged the concept of body tilting to compensate for cant deficiency. Experiments had been conducted in the USA in 1942 where the tilt was induced by altering the stiffness of the suspension, and the French followed this with their own tests in 1947–48. Trials took place between Paris and Etampes with a compartment suspended inside a coach which was whisked through 800 metre radius curves at 160km/h. These trials proved that uncompensated lateral acceleration in the plane of the floor of the compartment was only a quarter of that experienced in the rest of the vehicle.

Similar experiments took place later in Italy with a seat mounted on a structure free to tilt within an ALn668 diesel railcar which ran through curves normally limited to 60km/h at speeds up to 100km/h. The earlier French findings were thus confirmed, and this in due course led the Italians to develop their own tilting trains.

In the mid-1950s, the Sotteville works of French National Railways near Rouen built a complete pendular vehicle with an egg-shaped cross section that tapered towards the roof; this ensured that when it tilted inwards in a curve it would not foul the loading gauge of the adjacent track. This kind of tapered profile is common to tilting stock around the world. The shape was particularly noticeable on the alloy-bodied Sotteville car because it was designed to tilt by as much as 18° to either side of the vertical.

The pendulum car boasted 32 seats, and it was presented to the press in December 1957 after an exhaustive series of trials. These took place coupled to a twin-bodied articulated electric railcar set – the original intention had been to build a self-powered tilting car, but this would have introduced complications such as current collection from a pantograph mounted on a body swinging to and fro beneath the overhead wires. The car was nonetheless weighted to simulate a powered vehicle.

One of the difficulties to emerge was that the pendular body did not right itself quickly enough to cope with S-bends, so that it was actually tilting the wrong way as it went into the reverse part of the curve. Sporadic testing continued for a while before the car was stored at Mitry-Claye; it moved to Saintes in 1979 where it awaited cutting-up.

There was little further development of tilting in France until the SNCF acquired a series of 90 *Grand Confort* coaches in 1967–70 designed specially to accommodate powered as opposed to passive or pendular tilting. These were designed to replace the earlier *Capitole* cars and to upgrade comfort standards on other prestige trains to the southwest. The 6° tilt capability was intended not so much to allow 200km/h running on the high speed sections as to permit faster schedules over the slower and more sinuous parts.

Experiments were carried out in summer 1970 with two types of hydraulic tilt apparatus fitted to a pair of *Grand Confort* cars. Numerous runs were made with each car on a section of the main line from Paris to Nancy between Meaux, Château-Thierry and Epernay. The test train was formed of a powerful Class 21000 locomotive, a generator van supplying power for the tilting gear, and an ex-Capitole car as a reference vehicle.

To be effective, tilting had to start as the car entered a transition curve. For this reason the accelerometer which sensed how much tilt was needed was mounted in the van two vehicles ahead of the tilting *Grand Confort* car; this allowed time for the filtering out of lateral accelerations not caused by curving and for transmission of the signal.

After exhaustive trials SNCF decided to ditch the whole idea, at least as far as locomotive hauled operation at 200km/h was concerned. The equipment was complex, adding to maintenance time and costs. It increased the weight of the cars, and required substantial amounts of auxiliary power. SNCF concluded that the money would be better spent on ironing out the curves in the track.

First candidate was the 581km main line from Paris to Bordeaux where it was relatively easy to upgrade long sections through flat country. A pair of 200km/h first class only *rapides* was introduced on the Paris–Bordeaux run in 1971 with motive power drawn from SNCF's fleet of aggressively styled Type CC6500 six-axle thoroughbreds. Eventually no less than 350km was cleared for 200km/h, and by 1984 12 trains a day, some offering both classes of accommodation in Corail coaches with modified brakes, offered a premium service to the southwest.

By the early 1970s SNCF had replaced the cab signalling with something much cheaper and pragmatically simple. By adding an extra warning aspect in the form of a flashing green ahead of the standard yellow warning, SNCF effectively increased the braking distance for a 200km/h *rapide*. By the time it reached a standard yellow warning, a 200km/h train was travelling no faster than other trains and could then brake to a halt in the same distance.

## Tilting trend of the 1970s

The French were not alone in their tilting experiments. The complete series of 72 Swiss Express coaches built in the early 1970s for inter-city duties on Swiss Federal Railways' Geneva–Zurich main line was designed to accept powered tilt apparatus. It was needed not so much for high speed running but simply to allow an increase in speeds through curves – no small matter in a country where straight track is a comparative rarity.

Four prototypes were constructed and the first delivered in 1972. Tilting of up to 6° was effected by an electric motor moving a lever mechanism in response to instruction from a gyroscope mounted at floor level near the vehicle centreline. Like the French, however, the Swiss concluded that the complexities of tilting gear were not worthwhile, and the Swiss Express fleet which had other unique characteristics such as autocouplers remained as something of a white elephant. They were withdrawn from front line duties in 1986 and relegated to push-pull trains between Lucerne and Zurich Airport.

In West Germany DB opted to test tilt on its VT614 diesel trainsets and also on the three four-car ET403 high speed electric units. The system chosen was rather less sophisticated than on the other trains. It consisted of secondary suspension air bellows into which air was pumped from one side of the car to the other as the train negotiated curves. The system was developed in southern Germany, where it functioned well, but when the VT614s were moved north, their tilt control went berserk. It was discovered that track geometry was not the same in the north because the lines had been built by different companies. The tilt controls were modified to take account of the different curve characteristics, producing good results.

On the southern side of the Alps Italian State Railways decided to pursue the idea of powered body tilting, building on the results of its swinging seat trials in 1969 and development work carried out by Fiat's Professor Franco Di Mayo. A development programme was authorised in 1970.

The Italians possessed two tilting vehicles dating from 1957 and 1967, but Fiat decided that a completely new prototype was needed, particularly as the future tilting train would operate at speeds of around 250km/h.

Construction of the Y.0160 high speed tilting laboratory car was completed in 15 months. Trials began on 11 October 1971 on the Turin–Asti line, which exhibits snake-like properties between Villanova and Villafranca. It was a single 3kV dc power car packed with measuring equipment and a tiny seven seat saloon. The problem of current collection was solved by mounting the pantograph on a 'castle' structure enclosed in pockets within the car and resting directly on the bogie; this ensured that the pantograph remained in the same horizontal plane as the bogie frame.

The Y.0160 had a tilt capability of 10° either side of the vertical, tilt being initiated by a gyroscope that detected the start of transition curves. It also featured a remarkably low weight of around 40 tonnes, giving an axleload of just 10 tonnes. To minimise the unsprung mass the two traction motors, each with a continuous rating of 375kW, were slung longitudinally from the body; each drove the inner axle of a bogie through a cardan shaft. Numerous trials were carried out successfully at speeds up to 250km/h.

The results were encouraging enough for Fiat to go ahead with a four-car train. Two pairs of cars each formed an electrical unit, and the first pair's maiden trip took place in June 1975 between Turin and Trofarello. Trials with the tilt gear began in July, and Fiat was sufficiently pleased with the results to stage a demonstration run from Florence to Chiusi for delegates attending the 21st joint congress of the International Union of Railways and the International Railway Congress Association on 2 October. The second pair of cars was not united with its sisters until 8 April 1976, whence began a further stage in the test programme.

The crucial test of any train is its performance in regular passenger service. The *Pendolino*, as it was immediately dubbed, offered 171 first class seats in air-conditioned open saloons and a buffet-bar. It retained the main characteristics of the Y.0160 with tilting achieved by vertical hydraulic jacks linking the bogie bolster and the car body. The eight motors were each rated at 225kW and axleload was increased slightly to 10.8 tonnes, despite body construction in aluminium alloy – the single-unit had been built in steel to save time.

It was not easy to find a suitable route for a lone four-car first class only train; it did not have the capacity for the crack Rome–Milan expresses, so it was pressed into duties on the Rome–Ancona route, utilising the *direttissima* (which we shall come to in Chapter 12) as far as Orte, with the tilt mechanism out of use and speed limited to 170km/h. Only on the 211km from Orte to Ancona was it able to demonstrate its tilting powers.

The *Pendolino* first saw revenue service from July 1976 to May 1977 with four trips concentrated over the weekend from Fridays to Sundays. The other four days were needed for maintenance, repairs and checking of the equipment. Availability improved so that it could run seven trips a week from May 1977 to September 1978, with Thursdays and Fridays spent recuperating. In 1979 it managed a six days a week service, sometimes running beyond Ancona north to Rimini. On several occasions it was withdrawn for lengthy periods to undergo modifications, but FS gave no indication of being so pleased with the *Pendolino* that it wanted to have some more.

Among the obstacles which FS had to contend with was an objection on principle by the railway trade unions to first class only high speed trains which attracted a supplementary fare. This was clearly contrary to the egalitarian tenets embraced by the more fervent left-wing unions, and the *Pendolino* was just such a train. . . .

Simultaneously with the *Pendolino*, Fiat had built in conjunction with the Spanish company CAF a nearly-identical twin for evaluation on the 1.668m (5ft 6in) broad gauge railways of Spain. Its bright yellow livery earned it the nickname of 'Platanito' which in English approximates to 'little banana plant', although its official designation was *Electrotren Basculante*, Type 443.

Completed at Zaragoza in July 1976, it represented an ingenious bid to achieve journey time reductions on the Spanish National Railways main lines where fast running was hampered by frequent curves of tight radius. It had an 8° tilt capability, allowing it to hurry through a 300 metre radius curve at 105km/h whereas an ordinary train would have slowed to 78km/h. Passenger accommodation comprised 116 second and 51 first class seats, together with a cafeteria-bar.

Like its Italian double, the *Basculante* had its traumas. The electrical equipment was the source of much frustration, while the preselection speed control did not perform as anticipated. Modifications included reduction of the angle of tilt. For a period it ran in passenger service on the Madrid–Jaen route, but it spent nearly five years stored out of use. It was eventually refurbished for use as a charter train, and in 1986 it was deputed to undertake gentle duty as a tourist train ambling between Madrid and Avila.

The *Basculante* had a rival too, in the form of a clever adaptation of the Talgo concept of short lightweight low-profile cars linked by pairs of independently rotating wheels which had been pioneered in the USA in the 1950s before finding a home in Spain. Four prototype cars incorporating pendular tilting were tested under a programme started in mid-1974; numerous trials took place on the Madrid–Burgos line, and on 4 May 1978 the test formation managed a sprint at 230km/h with a party of Spanish and Mexican railway executives aboard. With diesel motive power, this was equal to the diesel world

Tilting Talgo. The unusual Spanish Talgo design permitted development of a version with pendular tilting; on running through a curve, a valve allows air to pass between the bellows, and the bodies swing outwards from the bottom by centrifugal force. Here the casing has been swung back to reveal the high level suspension after the first Paris–Madrid Talgo had arrived at Paris-Austerlitz on 25 May 1981. *Author*

Broad-gauge Basculante. Spain's *Basculante* tilting train was a broad-gauge copy of Fiat's *Pendolino* in Italy. (Compare with page 148)

record attained by Britain's prototype High Speed Train in 1973.

Tilting was achieved by raising the air-bag secondary suspension on pillars to roof height. When a valve was opened allowing air to pass between the bellows, the body swung naturally outwards by centrifugal force. The valves are closed at low speed to stop the cars swinging when negotiating pointwork. The arrangement worked well, and a fleet of 132 day and 56 sleeping cars built by Patentes Talgo entered service in 1980. With some reservations, French National Railways agreed to run a gauge-convertible version of the Talgo Pendular as a through Madrid–Paris service from May 1981 which shaved over 2hr off the previous best timing to give a 12hr 55min trip at an average speed of 106km/h over a distance of 1,368km. Although the Talgo clearly has potential to run faster, it is limited to 160km/h on SNCF's speedway from Bordeaux to Paris.

Apart from the Talgo, only one other fleet of tilting trains in the world has so far functioned successfully in commercial service, and that is the 1,067mm gauge Series 381 electric multiple-unit introduced by Japanese National Railways in 1973. This was based on experiments with a three-car articulated trainset of Type 591 which had been converted for tilting tests in 1971. On the 381 up to 5° of tilt is possible with the passive pendular system, but speed is limited to 120km/h on the tortuous Nagoya–Nagano line and on one or two other services. JNR is however experimenting with active tilt using air cylinders to augment the pendular system, the intention being to raise speeds to 130km/h.

Tilting is also being canvassed by Norwegian State Railways on the Oslo–Trondheim run where maximum speed is 130km/h and sharp curves proliferate.

In neighbouring Sweden the state railway and its local supplier Asea experimented with tilting in the early 1970s. Plans for a high speed tilting EMU took a long time to mature, but they culminated in 1983 when tenders were suddenly called for three tilting trains. However, neither Asea nor any other manufacturer could meet the specification, and new tenders were issued. In 1986 Swedish State Railways placed an order with Asea for 20 six-car Type X2 trainsets that are due to enter service in 1989 on the 458km Stockholm–Gothenburg run at speeds up to 200km/h. Journey times are likely to be cut from a fastest of 3hr 56min in 1986 to just 3hr.

In the meantime we must look at the most famous tilting train of all. It is the saddest tale in recent railway history, no more so than for British Rail which pinned so many hopes on the potential of its wayward child.

# 5

# BRITISH BRAINCHILD FAILS TO QUALIFY

The Advanced Passenger Train was the cornerstone of British Rail's Inter-City strategy throughout the 1970s. Had BR's plans reached fruition, APTs running at up to 250km/h would now be whisking Inter-City passengers along Britain's rail arteries in what the train's protagonists liked to call 'squadron service'.

But railways are a conservative business, and the innovative APT oozing with technological goodies was anathema to the traditionalist school in BR management. They believed it a waste of time, money and effort, resenting it as an intrusion in their domain. They fought it behind the scenes, undoubtedly contributing to its ultimate downfall.

The APT imbroglio was exacerbated by a stream of wild statements crediting the train with achievements that were little short of science fiction. Typical was the crassness of a glossy publicity brochure asserting that 'Inter-City APT marks the biggest single advance in improved train performance achieved by any railway in the world'. Back in 1971, Dr Sydney Jones, BR's board member for engineering & research had talked openly of 'the 400km/h version of APT' – and the experimental train had not even turned a wheel.

It would be easy to continue, and it is just as easy to be wise after the event. But the official line was that all was hunky-dory, even when it was obvious that fingers were being badly burnt.

From drawingboard to scrapheap spanned nearly two decades. In April 1967 BR's Derby research division launched a prospectus for a technically advanced train powered by gas turbines. Tiny inside frame bogies with a 1.5 metre wheelbase and wheelsets whose flanges would not touch the rails when curving would incorporate suspension with powered body tilting. This combination, suggested Derby, would help the train run on existing track at speeds up to 50 per cent faster than conventional trains – at no extra cost. Much of the technology, including the turbines and lightweight body structures, was rooted in the aerospace industry, reflecting the background of scientists at Derby who had previously worked in aircraft design.

The advanced train concept rested on research into the complex wheel–rail relationship. Central to the design was scientific proof that wheelset instability at high speeds could be overcome by correct choice and combination of wheel conicity and suspension.

BR at that time perceived the need to improve Inter-City services in both the medium and long term. Japan's bullet trains had given inter-city rail travel a substantial fillip, and some news of the advent of 200km/h commercial operations in Western Europe had crossed the English Channel. Studies were put in hand to see what, if anything, should be done on BR. Proponents of high speed running pointed to the phenomenal success of 160km/h electric trains introduced on main line services out of Euston in 1966 and the earlier achievements of the Deltics on the East Coast route.

Predictably, the ensuing report said that a British shinkansen was out of the question, and BR chose to implement the Derby stratagem as a cheaper way of achieving the same objective. The high speed tilting train seemed ideal for the sinuous West Coast route, and BR planned to have prototypes in passenger service by 1974.

In 1968 the government agreed to share the development cost of a research project termed the Advanced Passenger Train. The way was clear to authorise construction of a rolling testbed, APT–Experimental, and BR placed contracts in summer 1969.

Derby had not been idle. An APT development workshop was under construction and a 21km test track was being primed for high speed trials on a disused line nearby. Engineers were working on a pair of skeletal bodies mounted on long articulation bogies (the original tiny bogies had been dropped, along with sundry other bits of wizardry), and these were being used to test the tilting and suspension concept.

## Experimental train

The skeletal cars were followed by the E train, a four-car articulated set consisting of two power and two trailer cars, all able to tilt by up to 9°. The original aircraft turbines were replaced by a bank of four 400hp Leyland turbines in each power car, Leyland at that time being deeply into a scheme for turbine-powered lorries. A fifth turbine set provided power for on-board services and instrumentation.

Transmission was to have been via a reduction gearbox and cardan shaft to minimise unsprung weight, but this had to be abandoned because it would have taken too long to develop; Derby settled for axle-hung dc traction motors.

Tremendous interest surrounded the project. APT's ability to run at 250km/h on existing tracks ensured that other railways kept more than a weather eye on the goings-on in Derby. Particular interest was shown in the USA where the Department of Transportation was embroiled in its high speed demonstration projects. These were meeting with a conspicuous lack of success, and APT seemed a strong candidate for US conditions where track standards left a great deal to be desired.

Sensing an opportunity, the Budd Company, wrestling with the ill-starred *Metroliners*, rushed in and signed a licence deal on October 27 1969 for exclusive rights in the USA and Canada to develop high speed trains based on BR's new technology.

New technology there certainly was. Apart from the tilting, which required sophisticated electronics, wide aluminium extrusions were to form the bodies, while an entirely novel type of brake was being developed. This consisted of a turbine wheel revolving in a fluid contained in a chamber in a hollow axle. The fluid could absorb tremendous energy in a short time, with the heat being dissipated in a cooling system away from the axle. Termed the hydrokinetic brake, it combined low mass with high braking torque and could stop a 250km/h APT in the same distance as a conventional train braking from 160km/h.

APT–E made a modest debut outside its birthplace on 25 July 1972, only to fall a victim of the Associated Society of Locomotive Engineers & Firemen which promptly blacked it as part of a campaign to wring more pay out of BR for driving high speed trains. The blacking lasted for over a year, foreshadowing a plethora of other disputes that plagued the project.

In the course of its short life APT–E underwent substantial modifications that included replacing the trailer bogies with a completely different design. Among its achievements was a dash that peaked at 245km/h between Swindon and Reading on 10 August 1975. The following year the train completed its programme of trials and rolled into its final terminus at York railway museum.

At quite an early stage in APT–E's trials Leyland decided it was not going to develop the somewhat troublesome lorry turbines after all, mainly because of their propensity for guzzling fuel. Had Leyland not agreed to co-operate with BR for the duration of the trials, the programme would have been seriously jeopardised. As it was, BR was already hedging its bets on electric traction.

The next stage of the programme was to build a prototype train to carry fare-paying passengers. Electrical equipment incorporating thyristor control was ordered for this train from Asea of Sweden in 1972 – which did not say much for the relationship between BR and its native suppliers.

BR wanted to run the prototypes between London and Manchester, but there was political pressure to run a service to Scotland, and in the end BR had to settle for the London–Glasgow route. Starting in 1977, three years behind the original schedule, four 14-car prototype trains were to run a prestige service in a 4hr timing. This represented an average of nearly 162km/h – in the same league as the shinkansen, but on a railway that dated from the previous century.

Not until July 1974, soon after 25kV electrification had reached Glasgow, did BR win government approval for its electric APTs. The Labour government was squeezing BR spending, and pruned back the request from four to three. In fact, BR was lucky to continue with the project at all – it narrowly escaped cancellation.

Meanwhile responsibility for APT was switched from BR's research division to the chief mechanical & electrical engineer's department, and development of the prototypes was put in hand.

During the early months of the prototype phase more experimental vehicles emerged from Derby. A pre-production trailer car was constructed to run with the skeletal trailers, and an old wagon was rebuilt to test the power car bogies. Because the tilting controls and apparatus on the prototypes bore little resemblance to those on APT-E, another vehicle was pressed into service. This was a surplus coach from a fleet built to pass through the sub-standard tunnels of the London–Hastings line – its narrow body did not foul the adjacent loading gauge when it tilted.

Each APT prototype was to consist of two 3,000kW steel-bodied power cars flanked by rakes of six lightweight aluminium trailers. As passengers were not permitted through the power cars except in emergency, this meant a duplication of catering which on crew costs alone made a nonsense of some of the other savings being claimed for the wonder-train.

The reasons for this ludicrous divorce were tortuous. A single power car would have trouble lifting 12 trailers over the Shap and

Beattock summits at the north end of the London–Glasgow route, so two were needed. They could not be marshalled at one end of the train because unacceptably high buckling forces would be generated when they were pushing. They could not be separated as they would then need their own pantographs, and the rear pantograph would not collect current satisfactorily at high speed from an overhead line of relatively simple design that had been disturbed by the leading pantograph. Had BR not been obliged to scrimp and save on the Crewe–Glasgow electrification, a more sophisticated catenary able to cope with two pantographs running at high speed might have been erected.

Nor could a 25kV busbar run along the car roofs because the tilting posed a problem for the inter-car links. So only one place remained for the power cars – the middle. Here they could be fed from one pantograph, with a single 25kV link between them.

There was no good reason why the power car should tilt, but so it was. The pantograph was mounted on a frame attached to two vertical rods linked to the bogie below, so ensuring that it remained parallel to the track. To minimise dynamic forces on the track, body-mounted traction motors driving the axles through a transfer gearbox and cardan shaft helped to keep down unsprung weight.

Although the two power cars gave APT–P a 250km/h capability, speed was to be limited to 200km/h because BR was not convinced that the hydrokinetic brakes could halt a train from 250km/h in a short enough distance under poor adhesion conditions. Apart from that, to go much over 200km/h would require cab signalling, something which BR had failed to develop, although passive transponders had been placed on the track to provide an indication in the cab of the special speed limits through curves that applied to APT.

In practice the prototype sets of 14 cars experienced adhesion problems on the northern hills, and when the day eventually came to launch the train in public service the set turned out was a rake of only 10 cars. Just six were available for passengers; of the other four, two were power cars and two were trailers reserved for the small army of technicians who seemed permanently attached to the train.

The three prototypes were built by British Rail Engineering Ltd at Derby. Only in mid-1977 did the first power car emerge. Another year elapsed before the mayor of Derby took part in ceremonies marking the roll-out of three trailers. More delays followed, and not until early 1979 was a formation of two power and six trailer cars put together. The delays stemmed partly from unfamiliarity with aluminium welding techniques, but more serious were the 44 industrial disputes that sabotaged production and testing between June 1978 and March 1979.

A break appeared in the clouds shortly before Christmas in 1979 when an eight-car APT–P formation attained the train's design speed of 250km/h for the first time. Reached during a trial run between Quintinshill and Beattock, the speed constituted a new British record, overtaking that set by APT–E in 1975 by just over 5km/h. With five days to go to Christmas, another test run topped 257km/h.

Despite this achievement, difficulties continued to dog the project. The third set was not commissioned until early 1980, and entry into public service had to be postponed several times. May 1980 was set as the final, final date for the trains' public debut, and BR wrote it into the timetables. Then disaster struck.

To commemorate the long-awaited event, *Railway Gazette* had scheduled a special issue on APT. Several articles and elaborate colour artwork were prepared for the main section of the May 1980 edition. On 18 April we were in the final stages of putting the May issue to bed when the phone rang. At the other end of the line was an anguished press officer. A few minutes earlier Ian Campbell, BR Vice Chairman, had climbed out of an APT–P set that had derailed at around 200km/h. It was far too late for us to do anything, and the May issue went ahead, but APT's entry into passenger service didn't.

Quite remarkably, the train had not suffered serious damage in the derailment which turned out to have been caused by the failure of bolts securing the two hollow half axles to the central chamber of the hydrokinetic brake; the bolts had been incorrectly tightened.

Needless to say, APT's debut was postponed again, and BR announced in July that the service would begin on October 5. On October 3 a press trip was staged successfully at 200km/h, but nothing further happened. BR confessed to problems with the tilting gear, friction brakes and other items, and all three trains underwent modification. People were also beginning to ask some fundamental questions about the effects of tilting on the passengers, not so much the problem of tilt nausea as that of standing passengers and catering staff being thrown off their feet.

Though sceptical at first, BR management had developed a kind of blind faith in its troublesome prodigy, and it actually got as far as submitting a request to the Department of Transport to spend £35 million on advance orders for a production version. But the prototypes had still not carried fare-paying passengers, and the continued blight afflicting their commissioning resulted in an embarrassing request to the Department to sit on the application.

APT alive. In this shot of a prototype APT formation of 14 cars on a test run at Beattock in Scotland the inclination of the leading vehicles is apparent. On only one occasion did the train complete a public run between Glasgow and London in its 4hr 15min scheduled timing. *BR*

APT dead. Squandered on a scraphead in Rotherham, a set of APT vehicles awaits cutting-up on 13 August 1986. It was the sad end of a sorry tale, and BR's hopes of a speed-up on the West Coast main line from London to Glasgow withered with it. *Keith Hacker*

Failure to put the trains into public service was a major stumbling-block. In the autumn of 1981 amid a blaze of publicity SNCF launched its TGV service on a new line between Paris and Lyon at 260km/h – the prototype TGV had been rolled out in the same year as APT. BR could wait no longer. A launch date was set for Monday 7 December with a single train making three round trips a week – rather like the *Pendolino*. On the Sunday BR took a shoal of journalists north to Glasgow, where certain members of the party went out in search of more refreshment after a somewhat liquid dinner. Departure was at 07.00 next morning.

In the dark the train hummed south and a breakfast of kidneys and scrambled egg was successfully served by the dining crew who assured me that they were not bothered by the tilting. Whether it was the smell of the kidneys or the hangovers, it was quite clear that some passengers were feeling queasy. I too was somewhat disconcerted by the horizon moving up and down, but it had not affected me on the earlier part of the journey in darkness. Apart from that and a surprisingly bumpy ride, which did not help the queasy feeling, the trip was superb with a maximum speed of 222km/h being attained briefly at Blisworth. Including scheduled stops at Motherwell and Preston and an unscheduled one near Carluke, London was reached in 4hr 14min. Average speed south of Preston was 164.6km/h. At Euston BR Chairman Sir Peter Parker was waiting with smiles and congratulations. There were hand shakes all round. Ian Campbell made some derogatory comparison between APT and TGV. But the euphoria was short-lived.

The return trip to Glasgow was marred by an apparent tilt failure, which in fact was a tilt monitoring device detecting too much lateral acceleration when the train went too fast through a curve. Although the tilt had been functioning, the device caused the six passenger-carrying cars to revert abruptly to their upright position, giving the impression of a tilt failure and damaging large quantities of glass and crockery into the bargain.

The tilt equipment was continuously monitored for failure because it was once thought that a car tilting the 'wrong' way on a curve might infringe the loading gauge of the adjacent track. Although examination of the London–Glasgow route had shown that the danger was non-existent, BR felt it prudent to install a failsafe device that returned the cars to the upright. Needless to say, this bogus tilt failure undid the good publicity of the up run.

That was not all. Next day but one the APT trip was aborted because of ice blocking air pipes, putting the friction brakes out of action. On the third day of public service, 11 December, massive snowfall disrupted services so much that APT got no further than Crewe. With a score of one successful run out of six in a week, BR gave up and withdrew APT from service.

That, to all intents and purposes, was the end. For a period the trains were available for BR staff and their families to ride. BR struggled desperately to improve reliability, but it was to no avail. Commercial management was suspicious of the trains and feared that they might do more harm than good. In any case, BR had lost practically all London–Glasgow business traffic to the British Airways shuttle which had been launched within a year of completion of the Crewe–Glasgow electrification in 1974. By the autumn of 1982 BR admitted that the trains would not enter public service, although they would remain in use for 'engineering development'.

Director of engineering Ian Gardiner insisted on 27 September 1982 that 'APT continues to be central to British Rail's Inter-City strategy and is expected to provide 60 to 70 per cent of passenger services on the planned electrified network we are all so anxiously awaiting.' He went on to describe something called APT–U, which bore little resemblance to any previous incarnation of the train.

Gone were the articulation and the hydrokinetic brakes – they were replaced by high-power discs not unlike those on the TGV which had been the object of ridicule on one occasion when BR engineers had come across them. Tilting remained, but by now tests were under way to determine how fast conventional non-tilting Inter-City trains could run through curves without undue discomfort to the passengers.

It seemed that the cant deficiency could be raised from 4° to 6° with no serious problems, and as a result the successful Class 87 Bo-Bo electrics were given clearance to haul MkIII coaches at 177km/h on the London–Glasgow run. The higher speed was introduced on 14 May 1984, by which time BR was inviting bids for a new type of high speed electric locomotive.

The APT–Ps continued to run on spasmodic tests, ostensibly as part of the development of the new electric locomotives, but the end was near. On 30th June 1986 a rake of APT cars was delivered to Mr. C. F. Booth of Rotherham, scrapmerchant.

Whole books have been written about APT, and more of the story will emerge in time. Perhaps the biggest problem was too much innovation on one train, but there is no doubt that weak management contributed to the woes. On top of that there was bad engineering, bad public relations, appalling industrial relations, and sheer bad luck.

## Diesel insurance policy

By a stroke of good luck there were some far-sighted managers and engineers at the start of the project who were aware that exploration into the technical unknown was bound to involve time and risk. BR therefore decided that as an interim measure a prototype high speed diesel train would be built to exploit the best of conventional technology. Such a train would suffice to augment speeds on the relatively straight East Coast main line and on the Western Region routes from Paddington to Bristol and South Wales. No-one at the time could have known how wise a decision this was to prove.

Thus was born the diesel High Speed Train which deserves a special place in high speed history. Authority to build it was not given until August 1970. It was completed in June 1972 almost simultaneously with APT–E, but was blacked for a year by the same industrial dispute with the footplatemen's union. Only in 1973 did the prototype HST take the road, with a labour relations cloud hanging over it.

Technically, the prototype HST showed considerable promise, scoring a world speed record for diesel traction of 230km/h on 11 June 1973. It nonetheless underwent many modifications before it was judged ripe for series production.

Each of the 27 production sets ordered for BR's Western Region routes to Bristol and South Wales consisted of two streamlined power cars enclosing a rake of seven MkIII trailer coaches, themselves the result of 1960s research into the dynamics of rail/wheel interaction and suspension characteristics that had spawned APT. Power was provided by a 2,250hp Paxman Valenta engine in each end car. To limit dynamic forces on the track, axleload was held to about 17 tonnes.

To accommodate the higher operating speed on existing lines without resorting to the expense of modifying the signalling, BR succeeded in developing disc brakes able to stop an HST travelling at 200km/h in the same distance as other trains took to halt from 160km/h.

On BR's Western Region the entire 40km between Wootton Bassett near Swindon and Westerleigh Junction north of Bristol was closed for five months in 1975 to allow the track and formation to be rebuilt to accept 200km/h in the following year. The job included rebuilding and blanketing the formation, and similar but less drastic work was necessary at seven other locations.

In 1976, nine years after the French and 12 years after the Japanese, the first production-built HSTs put Britain among the elite of railways that carried passengers at 200km/h. The Germans had long since throttled back to 160km/h, meaning that Britain was one of just three railways in the 200 club.

Meanwhile the labour relations cloud had burst, drenching the prospects for low-cost high speed operations on BR. In one of several moments of weakness the British Railways Board had agreed that two fully-qualified drivers would be rostered for all workings over 160km/h.

The production HST had no gimmicks, no tilting and no frills, but it worked. The streamlined nose proffered the touch of glamour that the marketing men needed, and they coupled it with the clever promotional name of Inter-City 125 (for 125mph). This caught the public's imagination, and despite unambitious schedules in BR's October 1976 timetable, the HSTs were an instant success.

The fastest 1976 point-to-point timing at a speed of 148km/h for the London–Bristol Parkway run was soon bettered. By autumn 1977 Western Region was scheduling 59 runs a day at point-to-point averages of more than 150km/h, with four exceeding 160km/h between Reading and Swindon. One of these represented an average start-to-stop of 166.2km/h, only 11km/h behind the fastest *Hikari* between Nagoya and Shizouka in Japan.

A second batch of 32 HSTs was authorised for East Coast Inter-City services to Leeds, Newcastle, and Edinburgh, and four more sets were added to the order in 1980. These sets had eight instead of seven intermediate trailers, including two catering cars.

An inauspicious run of the first *Flying Scotsman* HST from Kings Cross to Edinburgh took 5hr 11min on 8 May 1978, but this was soon forgotten as the trains began to show their paces on the long stretches of the East Coast main line cleared for 200km/h. Seats were in short supply as popularity of the new trains soared from strength to strength.

In 1977 HSTs shot BR ahead of the SNCF in the world speed stakes. Frequent two-class HSTs outpaced the French first-class only *Aquitaine*, *Etendard* and *Capitole* TEEs which had held sway behind the bullet trains since the late 1960s. Further HST accelerations followed as the East Coast services bedded in. By 1979 Edinburgh was only 4hr 37min away from London, while two workings between Stevenage and Peterborough were timed at a start-to-stop average of 171.4km/h. Before electrification of the East Coast route started in 1984 HSTs were booked to cover the Kings Cross–Edinburgh trip in a mere 4½hr – an average of 140.4km/h for a 632km journey including one stop at Newcastle.

In due course more HSTs were purchased for the West of England route to Devon and Cornwall – where the scope for 200km/h running was distinctly limited, although the rapid acceleration from speed restricted curves nevertheless produced worthwhile cuts in journey time – and for the cross-country routes from the northeast to the southwest. The fleet eventually numbered 95, the last set being turned out in 1982.

Success is always bought at a price, and the cost in the case of the HSTs was in maintenance. With some of the most punishing duties ever demanded of a diesel engine for rail traction, it was not surprising that problems emerged – cylinder head fractures, difficulties with turbochargers and exhaust manifolds being those that attracted most attention. BR and its suppliers exchanged acrimonious correspondence, but together they persevered to keep the trains running.

As BR struggled under government strictures to make its Inter-City services profitable, the HSTs were juggled from one route to another, with some of the East Coast fleet working on the old Midland main line from St Pancras to Leicester, Nottingham and Sheffield. Here though they did not run at 200km/h, but at 160km/h – allowing a reasonably fast service without the expense of rostering two drivers for every turn.

HSTs, now probably past the apogee of their career as BR extends 25kV wires north towards Edinburgh, have served BR well in the absence of APT. At one stage BR even ordered an electric version, but continued indecision in its high-speed traction policy resulted in the order being cancelled shortly after it was placed.

## Inter-City XPT

The HST will go down in railway history as a remarkable train, being the only diesel in the world to operate regular services at 200km/h. A lasting tribute was paid by the Australians, who found it good enough to build their own version, Inter-City XPT.

In 1979 New South Wales was sufficiently impressed to ask local supplier Commonwealth Engineering to build four XPTs, and in April 1980 the company signed a deal with BR's consulting arm Transmark for access to HST know-how. Each XPT comprised two power cars and five stainless-steel trailers which were an advance on BR's MkIII design in that they had inward instead of outward swinging doors and second class seats which lined up with the windows; a bogie better suited to Australian track than BR's BT10 was also

Diesel dividend. BR's decision to develop a diesel fall-back for the APT paid off handsomely. The InterCity 125 High Speed Trains are the only diesels in the world to run at 200km/h, although their speed potential is not exploited on the Nottingham–St Pancras route where this photograph was taken in March 1987. *Dr W A Sharman*

HST clone. The origin of the Comeng-built XPT in New South Wales is evident from the front end; like its twin, it quickly seduced passengers with its image of speed. It is not only in England that high speed trains co-exist with archaic signalling. *John Dunn – Comeng*

fitted. Power cars on the other hand were almost carbon copies of their English cousins, although they were slightly shorter and lighter; the Paxman Valenta engines were downrated from 2,250 to 1,980hp to cope with Australian conditions.

The first XPT power car and trailer were handed over to New South Wales Premier Neville Wran on 24 August 1981, less than three weeks before an election. Scorn had been poured on Wran's ideas about high speed passenger trains ever since he had announced them in 1979. Seizing the opportunity to prove his opponents wrong, he commandeered the two XPT vehicles and had them tour New South Wales at high speed. Although the power car was only geared for 160km/h, this did not stop it being flogged up to 183km/h between Albury and Wagga Wagga before any proper trial runs had been carried out. It was a new Australian record.

With their ability to accelerate quickly and storm up steep grades, the XPTs were an immediate success. Two more sets were ordered, and by mid-1986 XPTs worked five services from Sydney, including a 4hr schedule over the 325km to Canberra. A further batch of cars is to bring the formations up to seven trailers, the same as BR's Western Region HSTs. It seems likely that XPTs or their derivatives will eventually work all daytime long-distance services in New South Wales.

# 6
# THE ELUSIVE CUSHIONED RIDE

The HST and the APT were BR's response to competition in the Inter-City market. The same pressure to cut journey time was felt by most of Europe's railways in the late 1960s. Rapidly growing motorway networks were exacting a heavy toll, and airlines were creaming off business travel. The threat from the air held particular menace for Inter-City trains as new generations of jet airliners emerged from the hangars. The European Airbus, for example, looked set to bring the comfort and efficiency of wide-bodied jets to short hops within Europe, just as the Boeing 747 had transformed intercontinental travel.

The boom in the air contrasted with relative stagnation on the rails – in the whole of Europe only a single stretch of line in France offered regular 200km/h running. Certain government circles were insinuating that the age of railways was over – the shinkansen and its magnificent achievements were conveniently forgotten. Investment was being channelled into roads and airports, not into new railways. There was token interest in high speed trains, but something with more appeal than the fusty old railways was beckoning.

It was the flying train or guided hovercraft. A vehicle hovering over its track would have no resistance to forward movement other than air, making it – in theory – ideal for high speed travel. In Britain Hovercraft Development Ltd, a company founded in 1959, had built some development models, but the French pipped THL, the later Tracked Hovercraft Ltd, to the post with the first significant hardware.

At the end of the 1950s the chief designer of Bertin et Cie, Louis Duthion, was working on ways of reducing the noise of aircraft engines when he stumbled on the guided hovercraft idea. Bertin seized on it and set out to prove that it could be developed at modest cost using techniques culled from the aircraft industry.

By 1966 Bertin was demonstrating a half scale model of his hovering vehicle which he dubbed the *aérotrain*. Running for 3km between Limours and Gometz-la-Ville in the southwest suburbs of Paris, its concrete guideway was shaped like an inverted T. The vehicle sucked in air and compressed it to form a supporting cushion underneath. In the course of its short life it gave joy rides to over 6,000 people. A second test vehicle followed in 1967, and with the help of rocket power it was forced up to a dramatic 422km/h on 22 January 1969.

This exploit focused attention on Bertin's invention, and it was not long before credulous politicians were advocating a hovertrain network. The first practical demonstration was to be a line from Paris to Orléans, and an 18km section at the southern end of the route was to serve as a testbed. Tall concrete columns with 20 metre beams were erected at a cost of Fr2 million per km over the fields near Orléans parallel to the main line railway that carried the 200km/h *Capitole*. Another Fr15 million went on *Orléans 250–80*, an 80-seat version of the *aérotrain* that had been put together for the Société d'Études de l'Aérotrain by a group formed of the airline company UTA and the Société Secan.

This remarkable craft drew scores of onlookers at Le Bourget airport in July 1969 before it travelled south to its parade ground near Orléans. For propulsion a pair of turbines drove a seven blade variable pitch propeller mounted in a shield at the rear, and a third turbine powered fans which pumped out compressed air to form 12 air cushions; three on each side were for levitation and the other six steered the 20 tonne vehicle by acting against the guideway beam's vertical centre fin.

Solid rubber wheels enabled it to turn on a flat area at the end of the test track. Being a child of the aircraft industry, the *Orléans 250–80* had two parachutes among its braking equipment. There being no adhesion, the designers had resorted to reversing the propeller to produce a braking force; they also fitted callipers to grip the central fin. If all that failed the power to the air cushions could be cut off, obliging the craft to 'land' on the guideway; special skids were fitted to allow for this contingency.

By this time the British were busy too. 1967 saw not just the launch of the APT concept but also the start of a flirtation with hovertrains marked by formation of Tracked Hovercraft Ltd. THL had a brief to prepare the ground for a complete high speed hovertrain system. By 1971 a 5km experimental box section guideway had been built at Earith near Cambridge, and a linear-motored test vehicle called RTV31 left the Swindon works of Vickers Ltd on 2 August. To collect power for the air cushion fans and on-board electrical equipment no less than five conductor rails were installed on the guideway.

Progress was slow, and translating the experiment into hardware for a projected route from London to Manchester or for a line to the third London airport then planned on the Maplin sands was another matter. On 7 February 1973 the Earith team managed to work RTV31 up to 167km/h – but that speed was approached every day by many of BR's Inter-City trains.

Belated realisation that a hovertrain network would involve duplication of BR lines (which would then lose much of their traffic) led the government to change its mind; Inter-City journey times were in any case to be reduced by APT. As there was very little to show for the £5 million spent on tracked hovercraft, just seven days after the 'high speed' run at Earith the government announced the end of the affair.

## America pitches in

Enthusiastic American entrepreneurs had meanwhile taken up the cause. Not long after the *Orléans* craft began roaring up and down near the town of that name the US aerospace group Rohr signed a deal with Bertin and the Société d'Études de l'Aérotrain giving it the right to *aérotrain* technology in North America.

Rohr built an air cushion vehicle for testing on a guideway at the Department of Transportation Test Center, near the town of Pueblo on the edge of the Colorado desert. It was one of three 'high speed ground transportation systems' for which the Federal Railroad Administration became responsible in the early 1970s.

Among the fantasies conceived for Pueblo was an evacuated tube in which passengers sealed in capsules would go so fast that it would probably be necessary to knock them out with a jab of dope before they set off. No-one ever found out whether loss of consciousness was essential for this form of transport as the idea was not taken too seriously by the pursestring holders.

A rival for the Rohr vehicle was unveiled by Grumman Aerospace at the Transpo exhibition in Washington in 1972. Initially jet-propelled, it was later converted for linear motor operation. At Pueblo it ran in a 5km channel shaped guideway.

The third experimental high speed vehicle under the FRA's jurisdiction at Pueblo was a linear motored car built by Garrett AiResearch; unlike the other two, it had flanged steel wheels and ran on standard gauge railway track.

Back in France, Bertin was fighting a losing battle. Despite apparent official backing for a scheme to build a 25km *aérotrain* link from the futuristic La Défense business centre to the new town of Cergy-Pontoise west of Paris, Bertin was going nowhere. As with THL in Britain, he had proposed linear motor propulsion to eliminate the environmental objection of using aircraft engines at ground level, but this did not impress the authorities when it came to investing large sums of money. In the face of Bertin's claim that an *aérotrain* to Cergy would cost Fr9 million less than a conventional railway and despite an incredible moment when he coaxed his craft up to 428km/h on 4 March 1974 his efforts were in vain. The Cergy *aérotrain* scheme was abandoned in the same year and an ordinary electric railway approved in 1976.

Bertin has left a permanent monument. The slowly crumbling guideway near Orléans is a unique reminder of his invention which can be seen from trains passing on the Paris–Bordeaux main line a few hundred metres away. In the words of Anthony Sampson the *aérotrain* had proved 'the most science fiction project on the continent'.

In the USA the Garrett linear motored vehicle slaughtered all records for rail vehicles on 14 August 1974 when it rocketed up to a still unbeaten world record for steel wheeled vehicles of 410km/h. But it was all to no avail. By the end of that year the Pueblo boffins had as little to show for their endeavours and for the $100 million they had spent as their French and British counterparts. Congress voted to chop the research budget, and America's hovertrains were consigned to the junkyard.

## Levitation by magnet

The levitation proponents were not easily dissuaded. Hovertrains that blast air around tend to generate unacceptable noise and blow up clouds of dirt, but another form of levitation seemed to promise no environmental problems. This was the magnetic cushion. A string of electromagnets under a vehicle on a special metal track can be energised to provide lift; both attraction and repulsion techniques can be used to support a vehicle in this way.

Maglev (magnetic levitation) was in its infancy at the time of the tracked hovercraft abandonments. Progress was most advanced in West Germany where the government's declared intention of having a new type of high performance freight and passenger transport system operating at up to 500km/h between Hamburg and Munich by the end of the century was an enormous stimulus for development. It was effectively an invitation to collect money from the ministerial research kitty in Bonn, and a race between rival schemes developed within the space of months.

A working model of a maglev vehicle dubbed Transrapid 01 had been built by Krauss-Maffei in 1969, and the company swiftly upgraded its experiments into full-scale hardware. But it was beaten to the post by aerospace and aluminium carriage specialists Messerschmitt-Bölkow-Blohm which presented the world's first passenger carrying maglev vehicle to the press on 6 May 1971. Those who rode the 5.8 tonne linear-motor powered vehicle on the 660 metre track at the company's headquarters at Ottobrunn near Munich reported that the notion of smooth riding on a magnetic cushion was an illusion – every joint on the track was both felt and heard.

Transrapid 02 from the Krauss-Maffei stable was close behind. In December 1971 it levitated on a 930 metre curved test track at nearby Allach where it later reached 164km/h.

But before committing itself to further development Krauss-Maffei chose to examine what merits there were in air levitation and pitted an air-cushion car, Transrapid 03, against Transrapid 02 on the same track. The experiment confirmed that far more energy was needed to levitate with air cushions than with magnets, partly because of momentum drag – the term given to the energy consumed by accelerating up to the speed of the vehicle the mass of air needed to supply the air cushions. The embryonic German air cushion train was laid to rest.

In 1974 the Ministry for Research & Technology intimated that MBB and Krauss-Maffei should marry their research efforts – both were based on similar technology using electromagnetic attraction. The two combined to form Transrapid-EMS, and shortly afterwards another linear motored vehicle with 24 seats, Transrapid 04, was launched on a new type of track. Towards the end of 1975 the 04 crept past the 200 barrier to a maximum of 205.7km/h, but substantial modifications had to be made to overcome a malaise with the linear motor drive and some serious structural vibrations.

To test all the hardware being engineered in West Germany Transport Minister George Leber had in 1971 promised a German equivalent to Pueblo at Donauried, not far from MBB's plant at Donauwörth in Swabia. But by 1975 the layout of the site was still up in the air, and well-orchestrated opposition from local residents and conservationists meant that a completion date was as far off as ever.

So the Transrapid-EMS team opted to construct a 1.3km test track at Manching. This was home to a component testbed called *Komet* designed to investigate maglev performance at speeds in the 300 to 400km/h range. To whisk *Komet* up to these speeds it was attached to a sled powered by steam rockets. This catapulted it along the first 300 metre section of the track where the sled detached. Measurements were then taken over the next 300 metre section, the rest of the track being needed for braking. *Komet* hit a sensational 401.3km/h on 19 February 1976.

Meantime the giant Krupp organisation had made a foray into the field by carrying out experiments with permanent magnets. In this case no power source is needed for levitation, but this advantage is offset by the weight of the permanent magnets and problems of inherent instability. Whereas the instability of the electromagnetic system can be controlled by regulating the current flowing through the electromagnet, the permanent magnet needs some kind of lateral guidance – like wheels. Krupp quietly withdrew.

More successful was a bid from Siemens, Brown Boveri and AEG. They erected a circular test track at Erlangen for an electrodynamic maglev system based on superconducting magnets. Superconductivity is the state of having no electrical resistance, which can be achieved in certain metals by lowering their temperature to something approaching absolute zero. In this state a very powerful magnetic field can be created, an arrangement well suited to levitation because the magnets on board the vehicle can be quite small. But refrigerating the magnets and maintaining them at very low temperatures is a major handicap.

Another difficulty is that the lifting force for this type of maglev vehicle is generated by currents induced in coils in the track by the vehicle moving over them. Thus the Siemens EET 01 test vehicle had to 'taxi' on 16 wheels before it levitated on its steeply-canted circular track. It first left the ground in March 1976 and attained 140km/h.

## Emsland test track

Pursuit of two rival maglev designs in Germany was pointlessly expensive, and an appraisal of progress concluded that development risks were lower with the Transrapid-EMS system. In 1978 the research ministry agreed that a full-scale test track should be built not at Donauried but near Lathen in the Emsland which was so remote that nobody could possibly complain. Into the consortium for the Lathen site were squeezed all the proponents of the previous rival systems.

In the meantime MBB, Krauss-Maffei and Thyssen-Henschel put together a maglev demonstration for the International Transport exhibition held at Hamburg in 1979. A 70 seat vehicle called Transrapid 05 carried 40,000 visitors on a 900 metre guideway during the 24 days of the show.

Soon after the Hamburg junket contractors moved out into the bog and heather around Lathen where they began erecting the first two thirds of a 31.5km elevated guideway on which was to run a twin section test vehicle, Transrapid 06. As at Hamburg, the Emsland guideway incorporated the linear motor and support windings on the underside of the top bar of the T shaped guidance structure. This was designed as a long stator linear motor with an iron core. The high cost of the track was to some extent mitigated by using the car-borne magnets for the dual-purpose of levitation and guidance.

By mid-1981 the single track guideway was rising on its A-shaped supports at Lathen, and in the early part of 1982 Transrapid 06 emerged from Krauss-Maffei's plant in Munich-Allach. The 122 tonne vehicle was eventually married to its guideway, but in 1983 a fire on board caused minor damage which set progress back for some months.

The first levitation tests took place on 30 June when Transrapid 06 was towed for a short distance by a lawn mower, the intention being to demonstrate the absence of friction. By the end of the year the Transrapid group felt sufficiently confident to invite the participants of a high speed symposium in Munich to visit the site. They were flown to Bremen and bussed across the north German plain to watch Transrapid 06 being levitated and moved at walking pace out of its hangar. Although they were permitted to inspect the interior of one of the sections, they were not allowed to ride, and some hesitation was evident in revealing the guts of the vehicle to the visitors, among whom was a sizeable group of Japanese – representing the only other country apart from the Soviet Union still left in the maglev marathon. (According to Tass, an elevated 200km/h maglev system with a prototype car is being built between Yerevan and Abovyan in Armenia, but weird tales of this nature have been put out by Soviet news agencies for years with no photographic evidence to back them up.)

The Lathen guideway incorporates two sets of points, one serving

Maglev myth. Magnetic levitation is not the panacea for inter-city transport that its promoters would have the world believe. The Transrapid 06 maglev vehicle in the Emsland in north Germany achieved 355km/h in December 1985, 26km/h less than TGV Set 16 nearly five years earlier. *Thyssen Henschel*

Points to note. A turnout on the Emsland Transrapid installation is a source of amazement to visitors. Junctions on multiple 'track' would pose interesting engineering and operating problems. *Author*

the hangar and the other forming the link into the straight section from the northern loop. This is designed to be taken on the straight at 400km/h, but in the turnout speed is limited to 200km/h. Both points are huge structures, 57 and 130 metres long respectively, and they take 15 to 20 sec to operate.

Transrapid 06 breached 200km/h on 4 May 1984, but the test programme suffered a further blow on 19 September when another mysterious fire broke out, burning holes 'the size of a football' in the side of one of the twin sections. Rumours of sabotage emanated from Germany, and a ceremonial inauguration of the Emsland site was postponed indefinitely.

Transrapid 06 was once again repaired, and the tests restarted; on 12 December 1985 a speed of 355km/h was attained. The ultimate target of 400km/h was thought to be unattainable until the southern half of the guideway was finished. This was due for completion during 1987.

Yet another experimental vehicle is being built for testing in the Emsland in 1988. The list is getting rather long, so something called the Transrapid 07 reference system is spoken of, although the next vehicle will be called Transrapid 06 II.

## Japanese experience

Maglev development in Japan was originally stimulated by reaction against the shinkansen and its noise problems, with maglev promoters promising silent transport at even higher speeds. Two rivals emerged, reflecting another bitter contest – between Japan Air Lines and JNR.

JAL began with West German technology in 1971, but by the time the first hardware was built in 1975, a different system had evolved. Trials first took place at the airline's research centre in Yokohama in 1976 when the first vehicle carried two passengers for a distance of about 200 metres.

By 1977 JAL had a 1.3km test guideway at Kawasaki near Tokyo on which ran a squat unmanned vehicle with a pair of shark fin tails angled aggressively at the back. HSST–01 was intended as a testbed for a future vehicle that would whisk air travellers to and fro between downtown Tokyo and Narita airport – the route of the abandoned shinkansen. HSST–01 was levitated by magnetic attraction with propulsion by a linear induction motor; it was worked up to 150km/h in March 1977.

In 1974 it was JNR's turn to investigate maglev's potential, the idea being that it would be a long-term successor to the shinkansen. A 7km test track was built at Mimitsu on Kyushu, where JNR hoped to reach 500km/h. JNR adopted support and propulsion using superconducting magnets, and a 13 metre long unmanned test car, the ML–500, was constructed in 1976–77. One advantage was the large clearance between guideway and vehicle at high speeds, typically 100mm compared with about 10mm on the West German Transrapid system using magnetic attraction. This makes the vehicle more tolerant of guideway imperfections.

On ML–500 the superconducting magnets are located inside cryostats on board, and the extremely low temperature of −269°C needed for superconductivity is achieved with liquid helium. This becomes a gas as it warms up, and it had to be recovered and reliquefied between trips; this inconvenience was eliminated when an on-board refrigerator was installed.

In February 1978 the JAL car hit 308km/h with the help of rocket propulsion, to be swiftly followed by the JNR car attaining 301km/h in March. The cost of both schemes was mounting significantly by this time and the Ministry of Transport began to take more than a passing interest in what was happening to its money.

In the following year the JNR vehicle was gunned up to 407km/h on 6 October, reaching a high of 504km/h two months later. JAL did not achieve anything so dramatic, and it lost the financial support of the ministry. JNR on the other hand grabbed the headlines with a spectacular dash at 517km/h on 21 December 1979.

Next, JNR rebuilt the guideway from an inverted T to a U shape by removing the central upright member and incorporating propulsion and guidance coils in new sidewalls; the levitation coils were left in position in the guideway floor. A three-section vehicle 29 metres long called MLU–001 was constructed to carry a human payload. By early 1986 the MLU–001 had amassed 34,000km of trial runs, after which JNR decided to build yet another vehicle MLU–002, with 44 seats. This was completed in March 1987.

Shorn of government support, JAL sold off its maglev project for ¥121 million in November 1985 to a company formed the previous month by nine of its employees. JAL had already lowered its sights and no longer held ambitions of a high speed link to Narita. Its most recent maglev vehicle, HSST–03, was a modest affair for medium speed operation; it was exhibited at Tsukuba in 1985 and subsequently at Expo 86 in Vancouver. JAL cited as the reason for abandoning maglev that 'it is now time to concentrate on safety of aircraft operation and because the company cannot afford to develop other means

Uncertain future. The trough-shaped guideway full of copper coils built for Japanese National Railways' MLU001 maglev test vehicle would be expensive to reproduce; note the lateral guidance wheels.

of transport.' This was a reference to the jumbo jet disaster in 1985.

Major technical and operating problems persist with both the Japanese and German developments. No maglev vehicle yet built can be described as a train; most have been single units operating on the 'one engine in steam' principle. As soon as several vehicles or routes are involved the question of moving them from one track to another arises. The complexity and cost of pointwork helps to explain why maglev will never take the place of high speed trains.

The truth is that maglev has no market. High speed trains can move large numbers of people as fast as they need to go on inter-city journeys, and beyond that aircraft handle long-distance travel with admirable efficiency.

The most telling comment I have heard on maglev was at a conference in Birmingham in 1984. Dr M P Reece, technical director of Britain's GEC, had this to say: 'If people all rode around on hovercraft or maglev vehicles, then the invention of the wheel would be a greater step forward than we are seeing today.' It is a sobering thought that despite millions spent on research in Japan and Germany a maglev vehicle has yet to carry a fare-paying passenger.

# 7

# GENESIS OF FRANCE'S SUPERTRAIN

While Bertin's star was at its zenith he floated the idea of an inter-city *aérotrain* from Paris to Lyons. This was an alternative to a project dearly cherished by the SNCF that originated about the time the shinkansen was launched. The French do not willingly admit to foreign influences, and it was said that a senior civil engineer on SNCF's Réseau Nord had been particularly struck by the design of the autoroute du nord between Paris and Lille.

Robert Geais conceived the idea of a high speed railway offering a Paris–Lille journey time of 1hr, and he put this suggestion to SNCF's director of research Bernard de Fontgalland. The research department had been formed in August 1966 by SNCF president André Ségalat who perceived that ideas would stultify if there was no forum in which they could mature. De Fontgalland placed the high speed dossier in the hands of his deputy, Marcel Tessier.

De Fontgalland later became secretary general of the International Union of Railways, a post in which he was succeeded by Jean Bouley, another senior SNCF engineer whose name will always be associated with France's high speed trains. Bouley relates that de Fontgalland's home was Lyons. This meant that he spent many hours commuting to and from Paris, the fastest journey on the old PLM main line being by the luxury *Mistral*. From 1969 onwards this TEE boasted a hairdressing salon as well as gourmet food and a lavish bar, but it still took 3¾hr to cover the 512km. According to Bouley, this was a considerable source of irritation to de Fontgalland.

A Paris–Lille high speed line would in any case have been hard to justify on its own, but the logical continuation to Brussels and the Channel Tunnel would have added an international dimension, effectively removing it from SNCF's control. SNCF turned instead to its prime traffic axis serving the rapidly developing Rhône–Alpes region. It just happened to be de Fontgalland's commuting run.

At once a feasibility study was commissioned into a Paris–Lyons high speed line. Two options were examined: an alignment with 1.5 per cent grades and minimum curve radius of 3,000 metres and a cheaper alternative with 2 per cent grades and curves of 2,500 metres radius. In the second case tilt-body trains would run faster through the sharper curves.

On 5 December 1966 the research department was given a formal brief to explore 'the railway possibilities on new infrastructure' in a project coded C03. The brief stipulated that, in contrast to the New Tokaido line, any new railways in France were to be compatible with the existing network. In this way new construction could be restricted to France's thinly-populated countryside, with access to cities over existing lines. A preliminary route survey confirmed that Paris–Lyons looked a good bet, and the department went ahead with a full-blown research scheme on 10 July 1967.

The first reports were produced in April and May 1968. They set out a Fr37.4 million research programme covering the following four years and recommended technical and operating parameters for the proposed line.

The justification for the new route was saturation of the old main line. Freight and passenger traffic had grown since 1960 at an average annual rate of 4 per cent, outshining all other routes. Line capacity was limited by two sections of double track in what was otherwise largely a four track route; on average, 250 trains a day had to be threaded through the section between St Florentin and Dijon, where peak capacity was 260 trains a day. Any thought of quadrupling was tempered by formidable cliffs and gorges, rendering the cost out of all proportion to the benefits. SNCF contended that the money would be better spent on a completely new line.

De Fontgalland and his team set out to demonstrate that a high speed line for exclusive use of passenger trains offered remarkable advantages. The old route would be left free for freight trains to rumble along at their own pace, while the whole pattern of passenger services between Paris and southeast France could be recast. As with the shinkansen, all the constraints imposed by running a mix of passenger and freight on the same tracks could be thrown to the winds; for example, no compromise on cant levels would be necessary.

Speed on the new line was the object of considerable research. SNCF accepted that 200km/h was probably the practical optimum for locomotive-hauled trains on existing track. But given a free hand to design new track and trains together, senior engineers were convinced that a considerable margin lay unexploited before critical speeds were reached.

As in Britain, research into the dynamics of wheel–rail interaction confirmed that bogie instability at high speeds was not insuperable. If the axleload was kept to 16 tonnes and unsprung mass held to a minimum, there was every reason to believe that regular services at 250 or even 300km/h were within grasp. As evidence it could point to the tests in the 1950s – some 400 runs exceeding 200km/h with relatively unsophisticated rolling stock and conventional track had been made in 1955–57 alone.

In this speed range air resistance, which increases as the square of the speed, is the largest force opposing forward movement. An aerodynamically efficient design would permit higher speeds without requiring excessive extra power, and SNCF set out to design a trainset that would consume no more energy at 260km/h than a *Mistral* formation at 160km/h; admittedly, though, the *Mistral* was not a typical *rapide* as it could load up to 16 heavy cars, two of which might be generator vans.

The 260km/h target just happened to be the same as that which the Japanese had set out to achieve on the shinkansen in the early 1960s. SNCF asserted that it was compatible with the goal of a Paris–Lyons trip of 2hr, with a margin of recovery time built in. But it took a long-term view and settled on 300km/h as the design speed for structures and track.

One advantage of running in this speed range was the so-called flywheel effect of kinetic energy. If this was brought into the equation, grades as steep as 3.5 per cent would present no obstacle to the powerful lightweight trains that SNCF's engineers had in mind. Further investigation revealed that such steep grades would permit a shorter route to be chosen as the line could climb over the hills, motorway fashion. At the same time a handy 15 per cent would be lopped off construction costs.

## Gas turbine power

In parallel with the new line studies fresh territory was being explored on the traction front. Back in 1964, parallel with thinking in Britain and elsewhere, the idea of powering trains with aviation gas turbines was being canvassed. Turbines were compact, lightweight and eliminated the problems of current collection. SNCF anticipated that turbine traction would permit journey time cuts on routes where electrification could not be justified and where more powerful diesels would have meant upgrading the track to take heavier axleloads. It also looked to be the ideal prime mover for the Paris–Lyons super-trains.

A Turbomeca Turmo III weighing about 4 tonnes and offering an output of 1,150hp was fitted in the trailer of a two-car diesel set by SNCF's workshop staff at Le Mans; the turbine drove two axles through a hydromechanical transmission, and axleload was a mere 12 tonnes. The set was coded TGS and fitted with wind-tunnel tested aerodynamic fairings to streamline the ends.

On 25 April 1967, a month before the launch of the *Capitole*, the TGS was sent out on trial. It clocked 581 runs at over 200km/h, with 252km/h attained on 19 October 1973.

The immediate outcome was the ETG (Élément à turbine à gaz) turbotrain which sported the same combination of gas turbine and diesel motive power as the TGS. An initial batch of 10 ETGs was pressed into service on the Paris–Caen–Cherbourg route in 1969–70, where they quickly demonstrated their athletic prowess, paring journey times by nearly 20 per cent. Within a year traffic was up by the same percentage, leading to an order for a second batch of ETGs. Before long SNCF was confident enough to dispense with the diesel engine, and in 1973 a faster and more powerful breed of turbotrain with no diesel back-up called the RTG (Rame à turbine à gaz) took over cross-country services such as Nantes–Lyons and Lyons–Bordeaux.

Meanwhile, the research division needed to gain a thorough appreciation of the problems of high speed running. It chose to build a pair of high speed gas turbine sets, one of five cars, the other of eight; the second set was to have body tilting. Tenders for the first set were invited from seven manufacturers on 23 March 1967, but the government havered until 1969. An order for the first train was placed on 11 July that year, and Alsthom unveiled the forerunner of today's TGVs at its Belfort plant in April 1972.

TGV 001 was a five-car articulated set whose brilliant orange livery immediately commanded attention. A pair of gas turbines in each end power car drove generators which supplied electric current to two dc traction motors in each of the six bogies, giving a total power rating of 3,760kW. The centre car was laid out as a dynamometer vehicle, the other two cars offering 34 first class and 56 second class seats respectively. Interior design and layout by former car stylist Jacques Cooper was extremely reminiscent of an aircraft, a sensation which SNCF at that time did not seek to dispel.

A novel arrangement was chosen for the articulation. Designed to allow cars to move relative to one another, to offer a sealed gangway connection and to permit cars to be separated without fuss, it consists of a pair of ring-shaped structures linked by a swivel joint, the whole assembly resting on the secondary suspension of the bogie below.

TGV 001 spent nearly six years dashing up and down various parts of the SNCF network, especially on the familiar racetrack in the Landes. By 1978 it had logged nearly half a million km, with 2,037 runs at more than 250km/h. Of these, 207 trips were at more than 300km/h. On 8 December 1972, only eight months after delivery, the test team recorded 318km/h on the speedometer.

Quite early on it became apparent that SNCF's continued concern about bogie instability was unfounded. TGV 001 had all the fundamental characteristics essential to run safely at 300km/h. As a result, the sister turbotrain with tilt, TGV 002, was never built.

An opportunity to investigate one of the options reserved for TGV 002 came almost at once. At the end of 1972 the first RTG was due off the production line. Temporarily reduced from five to three cars, RTG 01 was appropriated to investigate the high speed potential of the latest bogie designs.

From December 1972 until March 1974 the first RTG made 82 runs exceeding 230km/h, on one occasion touching a peak of 260km/h. Careful monitoring of ride behaviour provided ample confirmation that stability at high speed was greatly enhanced by lighter bogies.

SNCF then looked at the possibility of shifting the weight of the traction gear off the bogies to reduce further the dynamic forces on the track. Another research vehicle was obtained, this time a 1.5kV dc railcar which was transformed by SNCF's workshops into a streamlined courser that belied its humble origin. Christened *Zébulon*, it began rolling in April 1974.

Featuring long-wheelbase Y226 bogies, chopper control and body mounted traction motors driving the axles through flexible cardan shafts, *Zébulon* was also fitted with eddy current rail brakes – another accoutrement earmarked for the stillborn TGV 002. They fulfilled their promise, but they had to be abandoned as they had the unfortunate side effect of heating the rails.

*Zébulon* proved the advantages of body-mounted motors and also the ability of electric traction to perform reliably at high speed. It was set a gruelling endurance test, often clocking up 50,000km a month. The 2.9 metre wheelbase bogies performed well, and a pair were soon fitted to TGV 001.

## Birth of the electric TGV

In 1973 outside factors had come to SNCF's aid. The oil crisis cast a shadow over energy policy, rendering railway electrification more attractive to the French government which, having no oil of its own, set in train a massive nuclear power programme.

SNCF immediately pointed out that the TGV scheme would save over 100,000 tonnes of fuel a year thanks to diversion of traffic from air and road to rail. Higher fuel costs also clinched the case for switching from gas turbines to electric traction. SNCF had already been pondering whether to abandon turbines in favour of straight electric traction using industrial current at 25kV 50Hz for the new line. In this case the trains would have to be bi-current so that they could continue to other destinations in the southeast over lines wired at 1.5kV dc.

The difficulties of current collection at high speeds had been mastered during a series of high speed trials on the Strasbourg–Mulhouse line, culminating in the development of a two-stage pantograph, so the switch presented no technical problems.

Under the original scheme some 80 gas turbine sets would have been built. Even after the decision to adopt electric traction the gas turbine was not totally excluded. Dual-system turbo-electrics would neatly solve the problem of running beyond the electrified network to reach Grenoble and towns in Switzerland. However, the quadrupling of oil prices altered the balance in favour of electrifying to Grenoble, while the addition of equipment to allow TGVs to take the Swiss traction supply at 15kV 16⅔Hz proved feasible provided that lower power ratings were accepted.

The case for running TGVs beyond Lyons was an essential part of the package which SNCF was working up to present to government. By serving Grenoble, Avignon, Marseille, Nîmes and other cities in southeast France the TGVs would be accessible to more than a third of the French population. Thus the line was deliberately christened Paris–Sud-Est rather than Paris–Lyons to emphasise its role in bringing the provinces closer to the capital.

## Selling the concept

Once the technical framework of the new line and its electric TGV rolling stock had been drawn up, SNCF had to sell the idea to its masters – some of whom were in favour of Bertin's *aérotrain*.

When the project first began to take shape France was under the thumb of General de Gaulle. His resignation in April 1969 led after a short interval under Alain Poher to Georges Pompidou taking the reins the following June. The first detailed study for a 'frequent service of high speed trains serving southeast France using a new Paris–Lyons line' was presented to the Ministry of Transport on 1 December 1969.

Pompidou, at first an opponent of the new line, was persuaded to view it in a more favourable light, and together with his premier Jacques Chaban-Delmas (who resigned in 1972 after a tax scandal), he supported the railway when it was under attack from other politicians. SNCF thus enjoyed in Jean Bouley's words 'complicity at the highest level'.

The politicians were naturally wary of a Concorde-style white elephant. Concorde had first flown in 1969, and the subject was very much in their minds. The project was accordingly submitted to the *Commissariat au Plan*, the French commission in charge of economic planning which has a very large say in the running of the country. It came under the scrutiny of a Monsieur Coquand at the *Conseil Général des Pont et Chaussées*.

Coquand's report was released at the end of 1970. It concluded that SNCF's pet project should be included in the sixth National Economic Plan which ran from 1969 to 1975. It also confirmed that the rate of return for the community as a whole ranked the scheme among the most profitable of all transport infrastructure under consideration at the time.

In SNCF's eyes the Coquand report was a crucial step. Being highly respected in political circles, Coquand was a man with a reputation to protect. More especially, he was not a railwayman. His favourable analysis of the Paris–Lyons TGV concept was thus doubly important because it was independent proof of the validity of SNCF's calculations.

So began a period of intense lobbying. Here SNCF was extremely fortunate in having André Ségalat as president. A member of the *Légion d'Honneur*, he had distinguished himself in the resistance in the second world war; after France's liberation he took up the position of private secretary to the Minister of Labour. In 1946 he became general secretary to the government, being appointed president of SNCF in 1958. During his years with the Fourth Republic he had got to know many men of influence, contacts he was able to reactivate and put to good use when SNCF was campaigning for its high speed line.

A decision in principle to go ahead was taken at the level of the *Conseil Interministeriel* in March 1971, but the scheme was to be postponed until the old line reached the limit of its capacity, probably around 1978. Accepting this, SNCF knew there was still much work to be done. In particular the exact route had to be finalised.

In the process of trying to find a route to please everyone between 4,000 and 5,000km of different alignments were examined. These included a spur from Pasilly to Aisy-sur-Armançon, so permitting a TGV service to Dijon, whose inhabitants were duly pacified. It is a remarkable tribute to those who negotiated the route with landowners that the final alignment passed no closer to a dwelling than 30 metres. SNCF also compiled a complete dossier on environmental effects, the result being a number of tiny bridges forming passageways for wildlife.

In the process of negotiating land purchase SNCF took advantage of an historical phenomenon whereby a peasant's land is parcelled out among his descendants, the result being that each generation has smaller and smaller plots from which to earn a livelihood. Once SNCF had agreed to purchase land from Monsieur X, it offered those parts of it not going to be occupied by the new line to the neighbours of Monsieur X, Messieurs Y and Z, either as compensation for the land that they were going to lose to the railway or simply as additions to their existing property. In this way the size of the plots was often increased. Landowners were in most cases well compensated, the peasants being, according to Bouley, 'crassly paid'.

## Project in limbo

From 1972 to 1974 a good deal of uncertainty surrounded the project. Political infighting was intense, and opposition groups gained momentum. The Ministry of Economy & Finances demanded that Coquand's report be revised and updated, and a new report was duly commissioned. This had the effect of confounding the opposition, as it not only confirmed the data of Coquand's 1970 document but also set 1981 as the target date for opening.

While all this was going on, SNCF was pursuing a strategy of dangling a bright orange carrot in front of the politician's noses. TGV 001 was undoubtedly one of SNCF's most powerful selling tools. Between April 1972 and June 1978 it was paraded on 154 high speed demonstration trips for politicians, MPs, industrialists and other personalities from about 60 countries.

Not only did SNCF use it to impress French politicians, but French politicians used it to impress their counterparts from other countries. It required only a little connivance to fix up a ride in the cab and arrange for a particular trip to be faster than the previous one, thereby giving a visitor the impression that he had taken part in a record run. Significantly, guests who rode TGV 001 included eminent figures from South Korea and Brazil – both countries where the French nursed hopes of building TGV lines.

In March 1974 the Council of Ministers announced that it was in favour of a new Paris–Lyons line worked by electric traction. But Pompidou's death a month later meant a new president, and if the project was to survive intact it was vital that the incoming president should not oppose it. In the ensuing elections Valéry Giscard d'Estaing won the presidency in a run-off vote and took office in May.

Fortunately Giscard perceived that it was in his and France's interests to continue with the scheme, and SNCF was allowed to proceed with the business of calling tenders for two pre-production trains while local public enquiries got under way along the line of route.

The last hurdle was cleared on 23 March 1976 when the government declared the scheme to be in the public interest, allowing SNCF to start procedures for compulsory land purchase. The project that was finally approved had a price tag of Fr2.9 billion, with another Fr1.9 billion allocated for rolling stock (1975 prices).

## 87 trains ordered

SNCF had the nod to place contracts a few weeks earlier, and Jean Bouley, who just then had been appointed director of rolling stock, made it his first job to order two pre-production trains and from 85 to 95 production TGVs on 12 February 1976. Builders were the two leviathans of the French railway industry, Alsthom and Francorail; the option for 85 sets was confirmed in November. They included six trains able to work via Dijon and Vallorbe to Lausanne in Switzerland and six with first class accommodation only for top business services between Paris and Lyons; these normally run in multiple with a standard two-class set.

The first sod was cut at Écuisses near Montchanin in December 1976. In all there are 410km of new railway. The new alignment leaves the old between Combs-la-Ville and Lieusaint, 29km south of

Paris–Lyons station, rejoining it at Sathonay, 8km north of Lyons. The branch from Pasilly to Aisy to serve Dijon and Besançon is 15km long, while a 6km spur further south beyond Mâcon gives access to lines serving the Savoie region, Geneva and Chambéry.

Mâcon is the site of one of only two intermediate stations, the other being on a greenfield site serving the Le Creusot–Montchanin–Montceau-les-Mines area; it is some distance away from all three towns, meaning that it is really only accessible by car. Had the new station been located a few hundred metres further south it would have been possible to provide good interchange to the Montceau–Chagny line.

There are no level crossings at all, and the line is securely fenced throughout. To limit its impact on the countryside it is twinned with the route of the A5 Paris–Troyes motorway for 60km and with a trunk road for 15km near Mâcon. There are nine viaducts but no tunnels, SNCF being conscious of the aerodynamic problems of trains passing in a confined space at high speed. On the other hand this meant vast earthworks, with a 40 metre deep cutting at one location.

Top quality rails inclined inwards at an angle of 1 in 20 to suit worn wheel profiles rest on thick resilient pads on the twin-block sleepers which sit in a conventional ballast bed. Pointwork is based on designs tested in the Landes in the 1970s, and the turnouts can be taken at 220km/h; the blades are so long that they have to be driven at several points along their length.

The line has no lineside signals. A cab signalling system provides the single driver in each train with a series of 10 colour-coded speed instructions ranging from VL (vitesse limite = maximum line speed) through 260, 220, 160, and 80 to zero which indicates that he must stop at one of the lineside markers positioned at the end of block sections. Each speed display is linked to a check speed which if exceeded results in automatic application of the brakes. Track to train communication is by jointless track circuits whose frequency is detected on board the train by inductive coils.

By early 1977 it had become apparent that the 1981 opening date was in jeopardy, and Minister of Equipment Jean-Pierre Fourcade indicated that the northern third of the route between Combs-la-Ville and St Florentin might be delayed by up to three years to spread the cost of construction. Priority went to the southern two thirds of the route on the grounds that it was here that the double track section of the old line was badly in need of relief. On 1 June SNCF general manager Paul Gentil announced that the northern third would not open until October 1983, but that the 1981 opening date for the St

Up and over. The remarkable 3.5 per cent grades which TGVs climb on France's Paris–Sud-Est line are emphasised by a telephoto lens. The French call them the 'Russian mountains'. *SNCF*

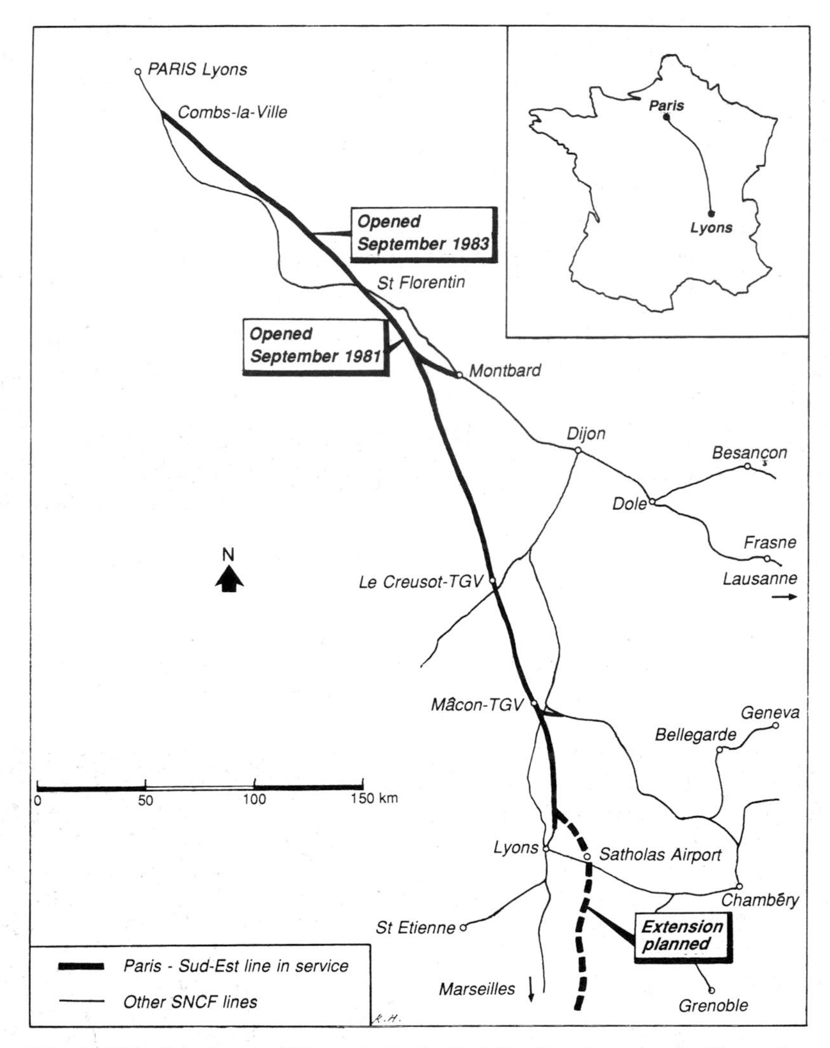


*Fig 1.* The first stage of France's Paris–Sud-Est line between St Florentin and Lyons opened in 1981, followed two years later by the northern section from Combs-la-Ville in the Paris suburbs to St Florentin. SNCF hopes eventually to extend the high speed line all the way to Marseilles.

Florentin–Sathonay section, together with the Aisy spur, would be held.

The first electric TGV was rolled out on 11 July 1978. The chosen configuration was two power cars with a continuous rating of 6,350kW enclosing a rake of eight low-slung steel-bodied articulated trailers; the end cars of this rake have a powered bogie next to the

Race to the south. At Paris Gare de Lyons on 27 September 1981 the 07.15 TGV departure (right) was the the first train to carry fare-paying passengers at 260km/h from the French capital to Lyons.

Spring cleaning. Workshop view of a dismantled TGV reveals the four sets of discs on a trailer bogie axle and the huge helical springs of the secondary suspension; both are clues to the engineering demands placed on the designers of the world's fastest trains. *SNCF*

power car so that six out of the 13 bogies are driven. Each Y230 power bogie has its own traction equipment module with thyristors functioning as a mixed bridge in the 25kV mode and as choppers when the train is running under dc catenary. On the new line power is taken from one of two ac pantographs on each set – a 25kV busbar runs along the roof of the trailers with special connectors between the cars – an idea rejected for Britain's APT; separate pantographs are fitted for dc operation.

Rheostatic braking is complemented by a bank of four chunky disc brakes on all trailing axles and clasp brakes to scrub the wheeltreads. A development of the suspension on TGV 001 has massive coil instead of secondary air springs, but this proved not entirely satisfactory and the entire fleet was refitted with air suspension starting in 1986.

In a length of 200 metres each air-conditioned set offers 275 second and 111 first class seats. Especially in second, the seating is rather spartan, while the blue and green decor gives a chilly tone. Passengers levelled harsh criticism at the cramped bar dividing first from second class seating and a more spacious and convivial counter and snack area is being put in as the sets are recalled for fitting the new suspension.

The first pre-production train was tested on the Strasbourg–Mulhouse line, where it was effortlessly worked up to its design speed of 260km/h on 23 August 1978 – within one month of delivery. It was joined by its twin sister on 19 December, and Transport Minister Joel Le Theule was taken for a high speed spin on 16 January 1979. SNCF then set about publicising the arrival of its new toys and arranged a regular circuit for top customers and prominent people which took in a brainwashing session in a cinema car attached to a Paris–Strasbourg TEE, a quick TGV trip to Mulhouse and back and return by TEE to Paris the same day.

Tracklaying got under way at Genouilly near Montchanin on 18 June 1979, with the first catenary being erected the following October. But all was not well at the plant in Belfort where the first power cars for the series-built trains were under construction. Delivery of the first set was delayed by a long and bitter strike during which emotions ran high enough for someone to feel it necessary to plant a bomb in the first power car. After the explosion a cache of molotov cocktails was discovered, and wild rumours went the rounds. The delay was fortunately not serious enough to warrant postponement of the opening, as SNCF reckoned it could get by with about 35 sets for the initial services to Lyons, St Etienne, Besançon and Geneva.

1980 also saw a dispute affecting tracklaying when police had to be called in to protect men working for contractors Desquenne et Giral. The company was attempting to cope with a strike by its mainly North African labour force by using Vietnamese immigrants instead, but there was considerable disruption with stone-throwing incidents and other unpleasantness. Eventually the police clamped down, invoking nineteenth century legislation that outlawed interference with train movements.

Trials with the pre-production sets continued, with one being slipped into service as the Paris–Lyons *Lyonnais* to gauge passenger reactions. As each series-built train arrived it underwent running-in on a circuit taking in both ac and dc traction. From September 1980 the trials were switched to completed sections of the new line, where preparations also began for Operation Antilope and the launch of commercial service seven months later.

# 8
# NEW LINES IN TROUBLE

Contractors' teams took less than five years to complete construction work over the 295km of the TGV line from St Florentin to Sathonay, and the remaining northern third of the route was commissioned two years later. This would have been quite impossible had construction not been preceded by thorough preparation that included early negotiations with landowners, not all of whom had reason to regret the arrival of their new neighbour.

One clue to the relative ease with which the final route was pushed through was obvious when I visited work on the new line near Montchanin in the early months of construction. On the way to the work-site my SNCF guide remarked that it was easy to tell where the new line was going to be built. All you need do he said, was look for the peasant farmers who owned new tractors.

Across the Rhine in West Germany things had not gone so smoothly, although in the circumstances it was not really surprising. In 1970 the Federal Railway (DB) had conceived an incredibly ambitious programme to construct not one but seven high speed railways.

DB had a legacy of main lines that no longer fitted the shape of the country after the 1945 partition. Before the second world war the Reichsbahn had a network of lines radiating from Berlin. Several had been upgraded to take the *Fliegender Hamburger* family of high speed railcar services, but nothing comparable was done to the sinuous north–south routes that wound through the central ranges of hills known as the Mittelgebirge.

DB's east–west oriented network did not suit the pattern of post-war economic development with new industries in the south relying on raw materials being imported through ports in the Netherlands or north Germany, and exports going out the same way. The situation was aggravated as industrial growth in northern Italy stimulated demand for north–south transits. Some of the traffic was absorbed by electrification which helped to raise line capacity, but many routes were overloaded.

DB saw no alternative to a radical restructuring of its network with a massive programme of upgrading work allied to a core of completely new railways (*Neubaustrecken*) that would bypass the worst bottlenecks and boost capacity where it was most needed. This programme would also permit inter-city schedules to be clipped, enabling DB to meet rapidly developing motorway and airline competition.

Priority was given to the 326km Hanover–Würzburg line down the eastern flank of the country. When the first sod was ceremonially turned on 10 August 1973 at a site just south of Hanover there was no indication of impending trouble, and DB top brass were confidently talking about completing the first three *Neubaustrecken* by 1985.

Apart from Hanover–Würzburg (which at that stage included a 50km branch from Aschaffenburg to Gemünden) new construction was also scheduled for a 99km high speed cut-off between Mannheim and Stuttgart in the southwest and a 150km direct route from Cologne to Groß Gerau, just south of Frankfurt. Of all the *Neubaustrecken*, Cologne–Frankfurt was the one needed most.

Between the sprawling industrial conurbation of the Ruhr and Germany's business capital in Frankfurt lies a tortuous crawl through the gorges of the Rhine. While tourists may gaze delightedly at the Loreley and the Drachenfels as the trains snake past, DB is acutely conscious that businessmen can ill afford the time of this distinctly leisurely train trip. Hourly Inter-city trains between Cologne and Frankfurt take more that 2¼hr for a journey that can be done in 1hr 20min on the *Autobahn* through Limburg.

Unfortunately, the Cologne–Frankfurt line was relegated to the back burner in 1976 when the transport minister decided that alternative alignments should be investigated. Plans for new construction were cut back to the section along the Rhine between Cologne and Coblence, and little further progress was made. In the meantime DB had been distracted. Massive opposition to the *Neubaustrecken* had sprung up.

Five years after the start in Hanover, only the original 12km was under construction. And although the Minister of Transport Kurt Gscheidle had agreed to release DM2.5 billion for construction of the Mannheim–Stuttgart line in January 1976, a ceremonial start being made in August that year, the chances of rapid completion were nonexistent. Virulent protests and bitter legal wrangling meant that further work on both lines would be delayed for several years.

There were several reasons for the lack of progress. The German landscape offers a striking contrast with that of France. As you look out of the window of a TGV cruising south towards Lyons long intervals go by without seeing any appreciable centres of population. Dotted among the woods and rolling hills of the Bourgogne are tiny villages and hamlets; here and there you may glimpse a bright modern tractor.

In Germany the population distribution is markedly different from the centrist structure of France. Medium-sized cities punctuate the landscape in a more even spread. Towns and villages crowd the remaining land, and the chances of steering a path round them for a high speed railway are small.

One of the main causes of delay were the strict planning procedures for large projects. The German constitution has built into it a number of safeguards to guard against recurrence of the failures of the Weimar Republic and to protect the rights of individuals. There is therefore ample opportunity for small groups of people to disrupt and delay a project of such magnitude as DB's new lines. DB found itself playing a helpless Goliath against determined Davids pledged to stop the *Neubaustrecken*.

Inexplicably, there has never been the same sort of hue and cry raised over the construction of *Autobahnen* – despite the fact that an incredible 140,000km of new roads have been foist on the West German landscape since 1945.

Two distinct processes have to be completed for the *Neubaustrecken*. First comes the land use and planning inquiry (*Raumordnungsverfahren*). This is administered by the provincial governments through whose territory the lines run. Proposals for different routes are worked out between DB and the provincial governments, and local authorities also have the opportunity to comment. It took five years for DB to complete this process for the Gemünden–Würzburg section of the Hanover–Würzburg line.

Next comes the planning confirmation stage (*Planfeststellungsverfahren*). The detailed proposals are presented to local authorities who are able to lodge objections. So are individuals. The intention is to finalise the route, but as DB has to take account of the wishes of hundreds of people it is a protracted business. Only after this stage has been completed can land purchase commence.

Throughout the process there is plenty of opportunity to procrastinate. The story goes that an apiarist opposed construction of the Mannheim–Stuttgart line on the grounds that his bees would get sucked into one of the tunnels every time a train went through. DB is said to have retorted by pointing out that this did not constitute a problem because the pressure wave of the next train entering the tunnel from the other end would push the bees back out again.

This ludicrous tale illustrates how far opponents were free to go in an effort to stop the lines being built. So successfully did landowners and lineside communities fight their campaign that neither Hanover–Würzburg nor Mannheim–Stuttgart will be completed until 1991. Not only that, but DB was forced to go to outrageous lengths to placate hostile towns and villages.

It has to be said that DB plunged into the deep end without taking sufficient soundings. Little attempt appears to have been made to test public opinion, and the railway planners were caught unawares. Only when much damage had been done did DB pedal furiously backwards, setting up information centres and producing mountains of literature in a belated attempt to explain why the *Neubaustrecken* had to be built.

DB's original new line plans envisaged they would be built to unusually generous standards so that lorries could be transported in closed vans running at high speed. Thus the distance between track centres was set at 5.4 metres, with the height of the loading gauge being about 6 metres. This meant that the width of a typical double track formation between the catenary masts was nearly 18 metres compared with about 11 metres for the shinkansen and the TGV.

But the outcry over the plans led to a searching reappraisal. Consequently, when the minister agreed to fund Mannheim–Stuttgart in 1976, he also indicated that important changes had been made to construction parameters for the *Neubaustrecken*.

## Mixed traffic routes

Instead of a top speed of 300km/h, the design maximum had been pruned back to 250km/h. The ability to carry lorries in closed vehicles had been sacrificed by whittling down the loading gauge, thereby saving 10 per cent of construction costs. The concept had a serious flaw in that it was futile building the new lines to a super large loading gauge if the existing routes were not similarly modified – a practically impossible undertaking. Nevertheless, the basic assumption that the new lines would carry a mix of passenger and freight traffic was retained.

This had important consequences. The French TGV line was dedicated to passenger trains designed to climb gradients as steep as 3.5

per cent and was thus able to stride motorway-style up and over the hills. In sharp contrast the German routes had to be engineered for freight trains too, which ruled out the up-and-over concept and obliged the route planners to accept large numbers of tunnels. The steepest grade acceptable for the German mixed traffic lines was 1.25 per cent.

Curve radii had to be large because a high cant suitable for high speed running would not be suitable for slower freights. DB plumped for a minimum radius of 5,100 metres, with the normal standard being 7,000 metres; this compared with 4,000 metres on the TGV line. The result was that there was little room for manoeuvre on the route – anything in the way had to be moved or flattened.

Another consequence was the need to provide banks of passing loops at intervals of 20km. These occupy huge chunks of land, adding enormously to the cost.

Even with the revised parameters the scale of work is staggering. The 4.7 metre distance between track centres is still 1.2 metres wider than ordinary DB tracks. DB engineers explain that the generous dimensions are essential because of the aerodynamic implications of trains passing in tunnels at a combined speed of 500km/h – something which the French had carefully eschewed on the Paris–Sud-Est line which did not have a single tunnel. On the Mannheim–Stuttgart and Hanover–Würzburg lines there are 80 tunnels totalling more than 150km in length, together with 384 bridges and viaducts with a combined length of 35km.

The numerous tunnels mean that all passenger trains routed over the *Neubaustrecken* will have to be pressure sealed. While all main line stock built from 1986 onwards will be fully sealed, older stock making up the fleet of Inter-city coaches will have to undergo a major refit. This has never been a major issue on the shinkansen because all the stock was built at the outset with sealed gangways, doors and windows.

Perhaps the best illustration of the scale of the work on the *Neubaustrecken* is the cross-section of the tunnels. The minimum cross-section of a two-track bore occupies 82 metres$^2$. To obtain this requires a much greater area to be excavated, typically between 120 and 145 metres$^2$ – an enormous hole.

Construction of such large tunnels in the irregular strata of the Mittelgebirge often ruled out excavation of the full cross-section in a single pass, resulting in the top having to be excavated and stabilised before a start could be made on the central and lower sections. Work was further hampered by deep clefts and fissures in the rock, while contractors sometimes had to cope with jets of water gushing into the workings at a rate of 350 litres/sec.

### Protest over noise

Then there was the question of noise. One of the fiercest complaints levelled at DB was the high level of train noise that the new lines would generate, with super-fast trains during the day being followed by a succession of equally noisy but slower freight trains during the night. It was noise above all that had damaged JNR's ambitions for more shinkansen lines, and DB found itself having to learn the same lesson.

Parties of lineside residents were invited to measure train noise for themselves. But DB's efforts to convince them that modern rolling stock was less noisy than older vehicles often resulted in demands for tall sound barriers along long sections of line.

Just south of Mannheim the new line to Stuttgart sweeps over a busy container and piggyback terminal before it passes the main Mannheim marshalling yard, hugging the western boundary fence. It then passes a suburb called Rheinau. Behind the village lies a prettily landscaped woodland where gently curving footpaths wind among trees that are curiously uniform in age.

So powerful was the opposition of the Rheinau inhabitants and their allies that DB was compelled to bury its new line in a 5.4km 'artificial' tunnel. A trench had to be excavated across what was to all intents and purposes flat country. The tunnel segments were installed in the trench which was then covered over and landscaped. DB's contractors then planted 100,000 trees to hide the scar on the landscape; the last tree is an oak which DB officials from the New Line Construction Office in Karlsruhe do not forget to point out to visitors. Incredibly, the contractors were obliged to nurse their embryonic forest for three years after it was planted.

Even after the tunnel's construction had been agreed disputes raged over it and DB at one stage had to halt the work. A full seven years went by from the time the first turf was cut until the moment when the builders finally downed tools. DB officials and the explanatory brochures peddle the line that it was necessary to build the DM110 million tunnel because the line passes here through a water protection area. This argument does not explain the biggest irony of all – the new line here is paralleled by the E12 motorway, a source of noise and fumes during day and night.

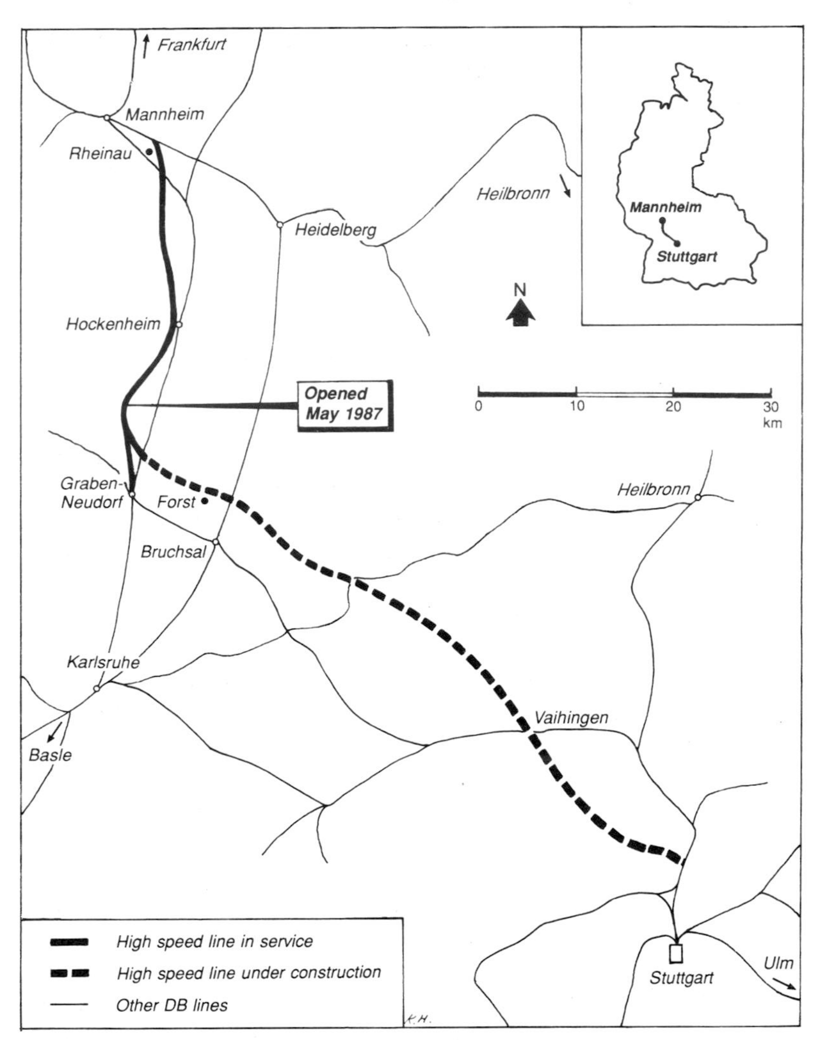


*Fig 2.* Construction of the Mannheim–Stuttgart Neubaustrecke in West Germany was launched in 1976, but opposition from landowners contributed to delays that mean it will not be finished until 1990–91.

Travelling south from Mannheim further evidence of the sops that DB was compelled to offer local residents is not hard to find. Entirely new roads have been built as trade-offs for the presence of the new railway. At Hockenheim, for example, a new dual carriageway bypasses the town next to the railway which is screened on both sides by sound barrier walls the height of small houses. Mannheim–Hockenheim, incidentally was the first section of the *Neubaustrecken* to open for business in May 1987.

Perhaps the most outrageous of all the structures that DB was forced to build lies on the edge of the Rhine valley not far from where the new line plunges into the Kraichgau hills. A small village with the appropriate name of Forst managed to have the railway buried in flat open country on the grounds that the villagers would otherwise be cut off by roads and railways on all four sides.

The victory for the inhabitants of Forst presented DB with an appalling problem as the ground here had a water table just 1 metre below the surface.

The method devised entailed driving 17 metre long piles each weighing 8 tonnes along both sides of the alignment. Next, half a million tonnes of sand and gravel had to be excavated, much of which was later used to make concrete for the tunnel sections. The resulting hole immediately filled with water. Special concrete formulated to set under water was then pumped to form a 1 metre thick floor in the trench, with frogmen being employed to check that it was correctly set. The water was then pumped out to form a kind of dry dock in which the tunnel segments were constructed. These were joined by waterproof seals and the tunnel covered over and landscaped. The cost of this exercise was DM85 million, for which DB could have purchased 15 main line electric locomotives.

Back on the Hanover–Würzburg line another hullaballoo bedevilled progress. Arguments raged for months over the route, with the towns of Kassel and Göttingen both demanding to be served by the new line rather than have it pass tantalisingly close along the Weser valley. Another factor that had to be taken into consideration was the need to give employment to areas close to the frontier with East Germany where business activity had been curtailed since the partition.

Although the 12km Hanover–Rethen section at the north end of the line opened for traffic in May 1979, it was not until May 1981 that a start was possible on the southern end of the route. The next section was expected to open in 1988.

### BR's 1970s Channel Tunnel link scrapped

DB was not the only railway to be fighting a battle over its new lines in the mid-1970s. SNCF was almost alone in persuading its masters of the need to forge ahead. Just across the Channel in Britain big trouble was looming for a new line planned to link the Channel Tunnel portal near Folkestone with London. Although preliminary work on the Tunnel got under way in 1974, a wave of protest against the proposed new rail link to London was swelling the tide of emotional opposition which every proposal for a Channel fixed link has generated since Napoleon's time.

BR was as naive as DB in its efforts to put across the message about high speed trains. APT was at that time looking promising and BR went into the Channel Tunnel project with visions of 200mph APTs capturing a huge slice of cross-Channel revenue.

But instead of extolling the virtues of a 3hr journey from London to Paris, BR found itself fighting off accusations such as 'Save Edenbridge from missile train', as one car sticker proclaimed.

BR's attempt to rush through consultation over the new line was in marked contrast to the careful negotiations for the TGV line to Lyon. As a result they were viciously attacked. A 129km route was proposed with a long tunnel under the Croydon and Balham area, Clapham Junction, and a London terminal at White City. BR fielded inexperienced staff to bat in the hastily called public meetings held at various locations along the route and as a result scored minus points as its speakers retreated under a hail of accusations.

Opponents made great play of a hue and cry about the noise of trains on JNR's shinkansen extension to Okayama which coincided with the British announcement of a new line to the Channel Tunnel. Evidence that the trains planned for the Channel link would be no noisier than BR's existing 160km/h expresses came too thin and too late. Like DB, BR was obliged to contemplate burying its new railway under the ground to meet the demands of landowners and lineside residents.

As time passed more tunnels were added to the alignment in a bid to satisfy the opposition, and the cost rocketed from £120 million to £373 million in the space of 15 months. BR's insistence on use of MkIII coaches that could not be accommodated within the restricted clearances on BR's Southern Region was one example of the failure of BR management to appreciate the economic necessities of the time. Even a last minute attempt to come up with an economy route carried a price tag of £250 million.

By the middle of July 1974 the government was echoing the rumblings of discontent and Prime Minister Harold Wilson relayed his desire to slow down the Channel Tunnel project to French President Giscard d'Estaing. The proposal to build a new London airport on Maplin sands had already been abandoned, and the Tunnel was increasingly being viewed as a grandiose project of the same ilk that threatened to empty the public coffers.

There was another factor too. In 1972 Harold Wilson had bowed to the wishes of the outspoken Labour left leader Anthony Wedgwood Benn and his anti-European friends by agreeing to hold a referendum on pulling out of the Common Market. That referendum was looming uncomfortably close at the start of 1975 and it was clear that the government could not be seen to be doing anything which was pro-European.

The Channel Tunnel was patently going to strengthen ties with Europe, and the impossible price for the high speed rail link presented an ideal excuse to back out. The unilateral cancellation announced on 20 January 1975 by Environment Secretary Anthony Crosland killed at a stroke that Channel Tunnel scheme. The project was not revived until the low cost 'mousehole' was mooted in 1979–80. From this the present scheme has developed.

# 9

# GERMANY'S CAUTIOUS CONTENDER

In one sense there is no hurry for DB to complete its high speed lines because it hasn't any trains to run on them – at least no high speed trains akin to the TGV or the Japanese bullets. When the Mannheim–Hockenheim section of the new line to Stuttgart opened in May 1987 the fastest trains were hauled by Class 103 electrics – the production version of the six-axle Class E03s that had hauled the Munich–Augsburg exhibition specials back in 1965. Their top speed is 200km/h, even on the new line, which is designed for 250km/h.

DB's first attempt to come up with something superior to the 103 was a streamlined multiple-unit designated ET403; three four-car prototypes were built in the early 1970s. Lightweight bodies with large aluminium extruded profiles were designed for 4° of tilt using the air suspension, but tilt was restricted to 2° because an arrangement for keeping the pantograph vertical had not been perfected. Thyristor controlled power equipment gave a continuous rating of 3,700kW.

All axles of the ET403s were motored to give rapid acceleration, and this formula allowed any combination of cars without altering the power/weight ratio. DB envisaged running formations of up to 12 cars on its two-hourly Intercity services that had been launched in 1971. But there were significant drawbacks. It was not quite as easy to add extra cars as DB thought as they had to be inserted inside the end driving cars and could not simply be tagged on the rear. Not only that, but keeping spare cars lying around was an expensive waste – each was effectively a small locomotive.

The ET403's attractive interior with compartment and saloon seating, full air-conditioning, 24-seat restaurant, train telephone and secretary's compartment did not hide the mediocre ride quality at high speed. This, coupled with the limited capacity of each prototype, led to their withdrawal from front line duties in 1979. They were relegated to charter work, 'sitting around for someone to hire them', as one chief executive of a German rolling stock builder put it. Although they ran for a period at 200km/h in regular service, they were clearly not what DB needed.

By good fortune another job was found for them in 1981. DB agreed with the German airline Lufthansa to operate them (for an undisclosed fee) as a feeder service four times a day between Frankfurt airport and Düsseldorf. Lufthansa staffed the trains with airline hostesses and DB provided the drivers. (Like BR, DB management had weakly signed an agreement with the trade union that trains running at over 140km/h would have two drivers.)

For their new role Lufthansa had the ET403s painted in the airline's house colours of white and yellow and christened *Lufthansa Airport Express*. They were refurbished internally to an exceptionally high standard, and the kitchen was altered to match an aircraft galley so that airline meals could be served at passengers' seats.

Once back in service, they were allocated Lufthansa flight numbers and restricted to passengers holding air tickets; check-in formalities were completed on board by the hostesses. An unusual attraction is that under some quirk of the operating regulations passengers are free to walk through to the 'cockpit'.

The failure of the ET403 to live up to its expectations left a vacuum in DB's Intercity strategy, just as APT had left a hole in BR's plans. Nothing better than the Class 103 locomotive was available for the foreseeable future, and DB found itself on the sidelines in the high speed stakes as the maglev proponents began to gain credibility.

The maglev schemes had been stimulated by the research programme funded by the Federal Ministry for Research & Technology which sought to develop advanced high speed transport. The programme embraced both maglev and conventional wheel-on-rail technology.

DB's failure with the ET403 did not encourage it to undertake another high speed research venture, and it was left largely to the rolling stock manufacturers to come up with proposals for hardware. As early as 1970 four builders had got together to discuss opportunities, but there was no point in pursuing plans without DB. The railway eventually agreed to participate, and in April 1975 all the parties put their heads together and came up with an outline concept for a train able to run at 400km/h.

This 'component test-bed' was to comprise a three car set with a laboratory in the centre of the middle car. Body-mounted underfloor traction motors were envisaged, together with a veritable bank of different braking systems including eddy current rail brakes and a form of hydraulic braking. This beast had a price tag of about DM45 million and was to have been completed by 1977. In the event the ambitious specifications and DB's inability to swing government policies in its own direction meant that the project was stillborn. The ministry's research programme did not permit such a train to be built in the short timescale proposed, while the biggest problem of all was having nowhere to run at the speeds being contemplated.

## Research sites

The ministry's plans for high speed trials had centred on construction of a huge test site for both maglev and wheel-on-rail techniques at Donauried. This excited considerable controversy among the local populace, and in 1975 it was reduced in scope and size. Whereas the original scheme envisaged 75km of maglev and conventional rail track, the modified project had only 57km and curve radii at the ends of the running loops were sharply reduced.

Arguments raged over the proposals until the end of 1977 when the government decided to scrap the whole idea because of rising cost and the unremitting opposition of local residents. Maglev research was to continue by extending an existing site at Manching and later in the Emsland, while wheel-on-rail research was to be relegated to a specially designated stretch of line owned by DB.

On 2 November 1977 Hans Matthöfer, Minister of Research & Technology commissioned a new railway research establishment at the Munich Freimann repair depot for S–Bahn trains. Although intensive efforts to develop maglev continued, this event marked the turning of a tide against which the German railway community had been swimming for some time. Realisation had gradually dawned that research into the wheel-on-rail mode would bring earlier results as DB would be able to make practical use of them.

At the Munich Freimann establishment was an extremely sophisticated roller-rig designed to investigate the ultimate limits of wheel-on-rail technology and simulate speeds up to 500km/h. It weighed a hefty 1,700 tonnes and was mounted in a hall the size of a small factory. Resting on its own suspension system to absorb vibrations that might otherwise be transmitted to the ground, it featured six pairs of powered rollers. These could be moved in and out, up and down, rotated and tilted to simulate all kinds of track irregularities. The Americans had previously built a similar rig at their Pueblo test site, but it was neither as sophisticated nor as successful as the rig in Munich.

In 1978 the government asked DB to designate which stretch of line should be allocated for the high speed tests. The traditional high speed test track was between Rheda and Oelde on the Hamm–Bielefeld line, but this was too busy for the fundamental research envisaged as engineers would require access for long periods without interruption.

DB chose a 23km section of almost unused freight line in north Germany close to the River Ems and not a great distance from its existing research centre at Minden. The line had the advantage of being almost dead straight and level. By coincidence, it was remarkably close to the site of the Transrapid consortium's maglev test track at Lathen. The Rheine–Spelle–Freren line was to be rebuilt to allow testing at up to 350km/h.

Track had to be relaid, level crossings replaced by bridges and existing bridges reconstructed. Work got under way, but progress was very slow. It soon became obvious that all was not well. By the middle of 1981 it was clear that the government was no longer willing to pay for the Rheine–Freren work to continue, although construction of the nearby Transrapid maglev track was at that time in full swing. Once again the railway community found itself manoeuvred into a defensive position with the transport minister accusing DB – with some justification – of squandering investment in pursuit of technical perfection.

It was a bitter blow for Germany's railway lobby. Earlier that year the French had pulled off the 380km/h world record and they were gearing up to inaugurate the TGV line to Lyon in September. DB's own attempt to develop high speed hardware had been castrated. The valuable work done on the roller-rig looked as if it might now be worthless, and a high speed test car completed in late 1980 was left with nowhere to run.

This vehicle was known simply as Test car 1 (*Versuchsfahrzeug 1*). Nearly all the leading West German rolling stock suppliers had had a hand in its construction which had been funded by the research ministry. It was unpowered, and rested on two bogies. Under the middle of the car was a special mounting for a single wheelset or another bogie, and it was this which was at the centre of the experiments. During trials the frame supporting the wheelset or bogie could be excited by flexible steering rods to simulate horizontal, vertical and longitudinal movements. All these movements could be measured and their effect on the wheelset or bogie analysed with the help of on-board processors.

With Rheine–Freren dead, all that was left was to exploit the possibilities of the roller-rig and to carry out limited trials on DB tracks. This situation was far from satisfactory, as not only a special test track but also a complete train was needed to take advantage of the knowledge that had accrued with the roller-rig. So in 1982 DB decided that if it was ever to have a new generation of Intercity trains it would have to fund some of the research itself. As soon as this decision had been taken, the industry agreed to chip in too, and all the parties met in Bonn on 6 September 1982 to agree what was to be done.

DB's share in the investment was set at DM12 million, and the industrial partners agreed to contribute a further DM16 million. The ministry's portion was DM44 million, bringing the total to DM72 million. At the ministry's wish, DB agreed to assume project leadership, and DB's research centre in Munich was allotted the task of seeing the project through.

A tight construction programme was drawn up with an experimental train due to be completed by the end of 1985, the year in which DB was planning to stage a number of spectacular events to mark 150 years of railways in Germany. At this time the start of commercial services with the French TGV was only weeks away. There was no time to lose.

## Intercity-Experimental

The task force opted to confer a snappier name on its embryonic test train to replace the cumbersome 'wheel-rail research vehicle' (*Rad-Schiene Versuchs-Fahrzeug*). They chose Intercity-E, the 'E' standing for Experimental.

Outline design had already been drawn up in 1981, and the shape of Intercity-E began to emerge. It was to consist of two power cars enclosing two low-profile trailers, one of which would house research equipment, the other being laid out as a demonstration car. A width of 3.2 metres was thought necessary to accommodate four abreast seating in first class, but the corollary was that Intercity-E would be restricted to DB main lines where the distance between track centres had been increased from 3.5 to 4 metres.

Right from the start it was clear that Intercity-E (ICE) was going to break new technical ground. On-board data transmission was to use optic fibres, eddy-current brakes were to be incorporated and a computerised fault diagnosis system built in. Novel drive equipment was postulated, together with three-phase traction motors. The trailer cars were to have two new types of steel-framed bogie, although there was talk of something which had never been attempted before – bogies made of fibre-composite material. Top speed was pegged at 350km/h.

Modern three-phase drives had been pioneered in West Germany and Switzerland by Brown Boveri & Cie during the 1970s, although the first experiments dated from 1963 when Swiss Federal Railways had asked Brown Boveri to investigate problems it was experiencing with traction motors when running in thick snow. The three-phase machine is an induction motor, so it needs no brushes and offers important savings in maintenance costs. It is well suited to rail traction as it allows available power to be exploited throughout a locomotive's speed range. It does however have a price, and that is the considerable amount of electronics needed to convert the electrical supply to the right type of power with variable frequency and voltage.

BBC pressed on with research and built three diesel locomotives with three-phase drive on a speculative basis; DB agreed to operate them in regular service under close supervision. Meanwhile, rapid advances were being made in semiconductor technology, and in 1976 Swiss Federal Railways commissioned a small batch of heavy-duty diesel shunters fitted with three-phase asynchronous traction motors at its enormous Limmattal marshalling yard outside Zurich; the same year saw six Bo-Bo electric shunters designed by the West German arm of BBC in Mannheim begin hauling industrial trains on the privately owned Ruhr Harbour Railway. In 1977 DB considered the technique to be sufficiently advanced to place an order for five prototype main line electric locmotives.

Known as Class 120, these were delivered in 1979–80 and subjected to a rigorous series of trials which revealed a number of imperfections. Major modifications were made, and only in 1984 did Transport Minister Werner Dollinger announce that the design was mature enough for DB to go ahead and order a production version.

Later that year Dollinger even went so far as to say that 'without the 120 – no future for the German Federal Railway'. This was an extraordinary statement by any yardstick, but however much it was open to criticism, it certainly expressed supreme confidence in the Class 120 and its three-phase drive. The ICE team decided that the same equipment would power their experimental train.

They also opted for something called the Um-An technique. Um-An is derived from the German expression *Umkoppelbare Antriebsmasse*. This refers to the mass of the drive equipment being decoupled from the bogie frame and transferred to the body. The idea was that at low speeds when the bogie is more likely to be rotating in sharp curves the traction motors would rest in the bogie frame in the normal way, with a flexible drive to the axles. At higher speeds when it is vital to reduce the dynamic forces exerted on the track, the motors would be lifted off the bogie frames by pneumatic cylinders connected to the body; the problem of bogie rotation would not arise because at high speed the train would be running on straighter track.

This ingenious idea was tested on a locomotive in 1982. The testbed was in fact a conversion of one of the original three speculatively built diesels. Finished in a startling blue and silver striped livery and with the letters UM-AN emblazoned in orange on a streamlined dummy nose at one end, it stole the show at the Hanover fair in 1982. During that year it was tested at up to 250km/h with the help of DB's specially geared Class 103 locomotive No 103 118–6 as the diesel could not attain this speed on its own.

During 1983 rapid progress was made with construction of the maglev test track in the Emsland and the first trials with Transrapid 06 were due to start in the following year. The group of manufacturers working on ICE was only too aware of this threat, while they were also keeping a close watch on developments west of the Rhine where TGVs were due to start the 2hr Paris–Lyons schedule in September. As they strove to translate theory and drawings into hardware they were obliged to make a number of significant changes.

Not least of these was abandonment of the active transfer of the traction motor mass from bogie to body in favour of a passive system. This achieved the same objective of reducing the horizontal dynamic forces exerted on the track, but with less elaborate equipment.

The other sacrifice was the wide body. With a view to ICE being able to run outside Germany, DB and its suppliers opted for a trailer body only 2.93 metres wide rather than the 3.2 metres originally proposed. The power car width was trimmed to 3.07 metres.

In March 1983 the DB directorate decided that to evaluate passenger accommodation in future Intercity trains it would be wise to add a fifth car to the ICE formation. They also agreed to pay DM4.6 million to cover its cost. Whereas the aluminium construction specialists Messerschmitt-Bölkow-Blohm of Donauwörth were building the first two intermediate cars, the third bodyshell was entrusted to Duewag which assembled it in its works at Krefeld-Uerdingen. The bodyshell was later transferred to Donauwörth for fitting out.

On 31 July 1985 MBB played host to guests invited to the ICE roll-out. It was a jolly occasion which saw the DB's Chief Executive Dr

Cut-and-cover. The Pfingstberg tunnel on German Federal Railway's Mannheim–Stuttgart high speed line was excavated out of flat terrain and then covered over to appease local residents. *DB*

Plane without wings. The German national airline Lufthansa found a use for German Federal Railway's redundant ET403 sets as a domestic feeder linking Frankfurt and Düsseldorf airports. The superb on-board airline service sets standards for railways to aim at. *Ralf Roman Rossberg*

Reiner Gohlke kitted out in a stationmaster's red cap to signal the start of the proceedings. Prompted by a shrill blast on Gohlke's whistle, the train broke through a symbolic wall of polystyrene boxes built across the doorway of a workshop. For the first time the white train with a pink stripe along the side rolled out on to DB tracks.

Photographs taken that day show the train from one end only, for at the other end was a humble diesel locomotive used to push and pull the train out of the works on to the main line. Power car Number 410 001 which had come under its own power from Munich specially for the occasion even had to be reversed ignominiously on a turntable to face it in the right direction!

Although 31 July was the official roll-out day, the first ICE power car had emerged from the works of Thyssen Henschel in Kassel on 21 February. So confident of the technology were Henschel officials that they said that ICE would be quite capable of running at its maximum design speed of 350km/h immediately.

Yet another ceremony followed at the works of Krupp in Essen on 19 March when power car Number 410 001 was handed over to DB; the Henschel car which had been rolled out nearly a month earlier was numbered 410 002. The position was complicated by the fact that Krupp had actually built both bodyshells, and the second one had been moved to Kassel for Henschel to fit out. The Krupp car was towed on 27 March to Munich Freimann where the train was to be based for acceptance trials, and the Henschel one followed a few days later. The trials began on 2 June and 100km/h was reached on the 26 June between Munich and Landshut. By the beginning of September 1985 the centre cars had arrived in Munich too and the whole train was assembled for preliminary test running.

## Record runs

Next destination was the research centre in Minden. From here the train was sent out on a series of test runs between Brackwede and Hamm. A deadline had been set for a high speed demonstration run for the press on 26 November 1985, and the test engineers were hard pushed to make sure that all was functioning correctly in the few remaining weeks. The first high speed run was made on 21 October, and in the next few days speeds in the 200km/h range were achieved. With less than a month to go, 250km/h was attained at the start of November. A brief period was spent testing bogie curving ability on the Steinheim–Springe section of the Altenbeken–Hameln–Hanover

Half a train is better than none. German Federal's Intercity-Experimental in reduced three-car formation roars past another test train on the Main bridge near Gemünden on the first completed section of the Hanover–Würzburg line. The other two ICE cars had been damaged in a derailment at 15 km/h in early September 1986. *Gerhard Schreiber – Plasser & Theurer*

line before the train returned to the race track between Bielefeld and Hamm.

Speeds were upped in steps of 10km/h, and the speedometer in the cab went past 310km/h on 19 November. At this stage the entire test section had to be clear before the train could start. The adjacent track on the four track section had to be clear too, and each trip was also preceded by a track inspection run.

On the day before the official presentation the test engineers notched up to 310, 315, 320 and finally 323km/h. On the next day about 90 guests were on board when the train began its run. Among them was Transport Minister Dollinger and DB's Chief Executive Dr Gohlke. The 300km/h mark was passed easily and at 11.29 the needle on the speedometer attained 317km/h. This speed was held for 5sec before the driver was obliged to begin deceleration. With only 8.6km available for running at more than 300km/h, the ability to achieve records was compromised. The 317km/h was written down as the official record, even though this had been exceeded on the previous day. DB claimed this as a German speed record and also as a world record for three-phase traction, being 52km/h faster than a run made on 17 April 1984 with a Class 120.

Passenger accommodation on the ICE set is aimed at a particularly demanding clientele. Behind the leading power car is the first demonstration car which is laid out as a spacious first class saloon with 28 reclining seats. A wardrobe is located in the centre and aircraft-style lockers are provided for stowing luggage above the seats. At the far end is a lounge and video area with eight seats arranged in a coupé round small tables.

Two of the seats in the saloon have the doubtful distinction of telephones and information screens set in the seat backs in front of them. Instead of payment by coin, a phonecard has to be obtained from the train staff, as must airline-style headphones for first class passengers. Electronically controlled information panels indicate reserved seats, car and train number and the name of the next station.

The second demonstration car has an 18 seat first class saloon at one end and a 27 seat second class saloon at the other. In the centre is a service area housing a catering module and toilet.

The third car is the dynamometer vehicle which is packed with measuring and monitoring equipment. It also contains a small kitchen for the staff.

ICE was paraded round Germany after the record run and in January 1986 it ran a few trips in commercial service between Frankfurt and Munich and Frankfurt and Hanover to gauge passenger reactions – not all of which were favourable. It was difficult for people to get in and out of the video coupé, and the in-seat telephones did not meet with universal approval. The headphones on the other hand were judged as a long-overdue improvement, but the wardrobe was not popular. Nor were the luggage lockers as they fouled the headroom over the window seats.

Next the train was put through a series of noise measurement and ride quality tests, during which the more conventional trailer bogie was found to perform better than its bolsterless rival with a coupling frame linking the wheelsets.

The fibre-composite bogie development was put in the hands of MBB which believed that its expertise in aerospace technology could be transferred to railways. Having long been a builder of both railway rolling stock and aircraft such as the European Airbus it stood a good chance, unlike US aircraft builders such as Rohr and Boeing who in the 1970s thought they could make trains too.

Main purpose of the intensive trials that then got under way was to define a specification for future Intercity trains, for which DB's marketing staff had coined the name Intercity-Express, allowing the initials ICE to be retained. Each set would consist of two end power cars with up to 14 intermediate trailers of two basic designs offering a total of 660 seats plus a service car with catering. Each passenger car would have a mix of open, compartment and semi-compartment seating. DB envisaged that one car might have a Pullman 'club' layout accessible by paying a supplement, but the economics looked dubious as the car offered only 37 seats.

DB also wavered over the eddy current braking proposals and reversed its earlier decision about the car width, settling on a non-standard dimension of 3.02 metres (the standard width agreed by the International Union of Railways for a 26.4 metre long car is 2.91 metres). It defended this choice on the grounds that many of the domestic routes where ICE sets would run were already fit to accept it, and any that were not ready would be modified by the time they entered service in 1990–91. DB also said that it had received assurances from Switzerland and Austria that the car width would pose no problems for through running.

DB planned to order a first batch of about 45 IC–Express sets in 1987 for use on three routes; Hamburg–Hanover–Würzburg–Munich; Hamburg–Hanover–Frankfurt–Mannheim–Basle; and Frankfurt–Mannheim–Stuttgart–Munich. The fastest Hamburg–Munich journey will come down by nearly 1½hr to 5hr 35min (an average speed of 141km/h including stops), with Hanover–Würzburg

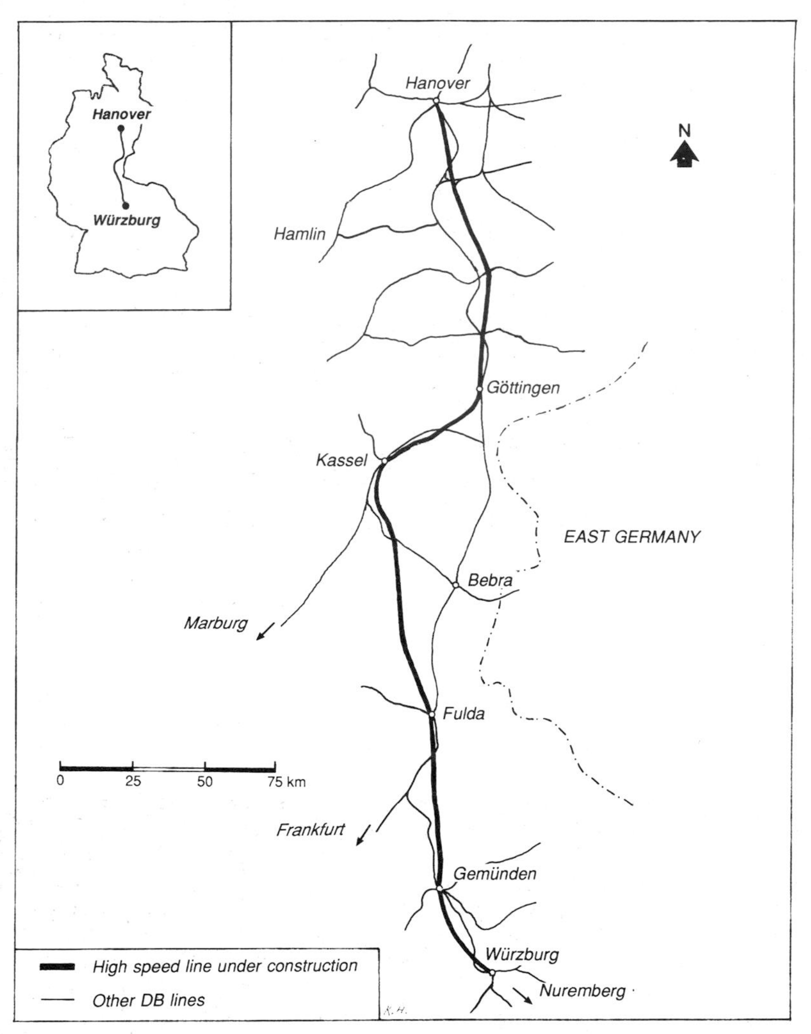


*Fig 3.* A section of West Germany's Hanover–Würzburg Neubaustrecke near Gemünden acted as the high speed testing ground for the Intercity-Experimental in 1986; the first significant section of the line will open in 1988, a full 15 years after the ceremonial start of construction in Hanover.

taking 2hr (163km/h) instead of 3hr 22min. Frankfurt–Stuttgart will be pared from 2hr 5min to 1hr 10min.

One of the most difficult design problems proved to be the sealed inter-car gangway connections which are flush with the outside of the train; those fitted to ICE were too complex and too expensive to war-

Target figure. The 350km/h design speed of the Intercity-Experimental features prominently on the side of the centre cars. A version of this Minden-Deutz 52 bogie has been retained for the production build of Intercity Express sets. *Author*

Near miss. Cab display of the Intercity-Experimental shows 5km/h below the design speed on a demonstration run on 17 November 1986. It was a German record achieved in the Mühlberg tunnel with the then Transport Minister Dr Werner Dollinger on board. *DB*

rant their use on a production version, so four alternative designs were fitted to locomotive-hauled coaches for trials.

The date neared when ICE could be run on the best test track of all – the *Neubaustrecken*. The first section to be ready was 28km between Burgsinn and Hohe Wart, near Gemünden on the Hanover–Würzburg line. September was the date set for ICE to switch over. DB officials in early 1986 were making confident noises about new world records, and the figure of 400km/h was mentioned frequently.

ICE arrived at the new test site and the first runs were completed successfully on 3 September with 260km/h being attained. Towards evening the set was being prepared in Burgsinn to return to Würzburg for the night when unsecured points moved under the train as it was switching from the new line to the old. Power car 410 001 was derailed at about 15km/h, damaging one of the drives and one of the complex inter-car connections. The power car and affected trailer had to be sent back to Munich for repairs, and a much heralded demonstration trip planned for the end of September was put off until 17 November.

On 16 November journalists assembled in Würzburg and were accommodated for the night in sleeping cars. At the crack of dawn next morning the ICE was waiting to take the visitors to the nearby new line. The car with second class accommodation was crammed with apparatus and only one car was available for the visitors. Once on the new line the train was worked up to 300km/h for the first lot of journalists and to slightly more for a second group, most of whom were French. In the afternoon prominent visitors included Transport Minister Dollinger, who was treated to a new German record of 345km/h.

Early on during the press trip any hopes of new world records were quashed by DB's head of the Munich Research Centre Theo Rahn; 'The section of line available is not long enough for world records.' Despite impressive acceleration and a rock-steady ride at 300km/h it was not possible to disguise the anti-climax. In the event even the train's design speed of 350km/h was not reached. DB could not even claim that the 345km/h was a record for three-phase traction, for a three-phase powered train had already eclipsed the ICE – in France.

# 10
# TGV GOES WEST

In the words of its communist transport minister Charles Fiterman, the Mitterrand government that took office in France in 1981 'worked for a renaissance of rail'. It was no accident that President Mitterrand himself inaugurated the Paris–Sud-Est line on 22 September 1981.

On such occasions there are always hitches, and this was no exception. The special TGV laid on to Lyons was 10min late leaving Paris, and en route a power and signalling failure threatened further delay. All the same, Lyons was reached in 2hr 27min, 13min less than the fastest booked time for regular services which began on September 27 – and that with only two thirds of the new line open! With the President aboard for the return trip, stops were made at Mâcon and Le Creusot, where there was dinner and speeches. Departure was 4min late, but everyone was satisfied when the Presidential TGV pulled into Paris exactly on schedule at 23.30.

With a spread of services to Lyons, St Etienne, Besançon and Geneva, the blue riband for the world's fastest trains was wrested from Japan after 17 years. The brilliant orange TGVs rolled at a maximum speed of 260km/h, giving a Paris–Lyons non-stop average of 169.3km/h (to Lyons-Brotteaux, which was replaced in June 1983 by a new station at Lyons Part-Dieu).

Even faster start-to-stop averages were attained between intermediate stations – one TGV was timed to cover 63.2km between Mâcon and Le Creusot at 189.6km/h. The fastest start-to-stop trip on the shinkansen in 1981 was by a lone *Hikari* between Nagoya and Yokohama covering 316.5km in 105min at 180.9km/h.

But there was an important difference. Whereas on the Paris–Sud-Est line 23 services a day were booked at start-to-stop averages of over 165km/h, there were no less that 292 on the shinkansen. Although the French had won the title of 'world's fastest trains', they could not compete in terms of frequency of service or volume of traffic handled.

In May 1982 SNCF added four TGV round trips between Paris and Marseilles, the fastest being the 12.45 from Paris which reached the Mediterranean in 5hr 33min with a single stop at Valence. On the same day the famous *Mistral* was withdrawn, ending many years of premium luxury service to the Midi resorts. More TGVs to the Midi were added in the following winter, together with an extra Geneva working.

Average load factor on the TGVs after one year was 61 per cent, with 5.6 million TGV passengers carried. Revenue outpaced costs sufficiently for SNCF to calculate that it would be able to pay off all the capital and interest for the new line and the trains by 1989.

An additional 20 power cars and 70 trailers were ordered in 1983. The French post office also acquired its own mini-fleet of two and a half TGV sets which on 1 October 1984 began working two round trips a day between Paris Charolais and Lyons Montrochet. The postal TGVs – easily distinguished by a bright yellow livery and trailer cars that have a large central door but no windows – took on a job that had been the preserve of Transall C160 air freighters. Each set can carry 61 tonnes of mail in special containers that fit snugly in the trailer cars, which have air suspension bogies.

In May 1983 SNCF lifted the TGV speed ceiling from 260 to 270km/h as extra kinetic energy amassed on the steep downgrades permitted the trains to coast longer, bringing a small but significant energy saving.

Inauguration of the 2hr Paris–Lyons timing followed in September 1983, being a start-to-stop average of 213.5km/h for a distance of 427km to Lyons Part-Dieu. In the following year services to the Midi were accelerated thanks to upgrading of several sections of the Rhône valley main line to 200km/h. January 1984 saw the first tri-current sets begin running to Lausanne in Switzerland under 15kV 16⅔Hz catenary, practically completing the spectrum of TGV services that SNCF had planned at the outset. Only Grenoble remained to be added in March 1985 after electrification; fastest timing was 3hr 12min.

A Lille–Lyons TGV running round Paris on the *Grande Ceinture* was launched in September 1984, to be followed by a Rouen–Lyons service two years later. Nice was added to the list of southeast destinations in April 1987, swiftly followed by a working to the Swiss capital Berne in May.

The TGVs were dramatically successful, just as the shinkansen had been nearly two decades earlier. Between 1981 and 1983 the number of daily passengers grew from 14,000 to 33,800, rising to an average of 47,000 in 1986; a record number of 88,862 were handled on 21 February 1987, a busy day for winter sports traffic. During 1985 nearly 16 million passengers rode TGVs, and the average load factor grew to an impressive 73 per cent. Loadings were particularly good on the Geneva run which had been cut to 3hr 30min, and Air France and Swissair struggled to maintain their share of the market.

## Mitterrand's promise

During President Mitterrand's speech at Le Creusot on 22 September 1981 he revealed that he had asked SNCF to undertake design studies for a second TGV line that would serve western France. In fact, SNCF strategists had turned their attention towards a second high speed line in the mid-1970s when it seemed as though the original idea of a route from Paris to Lille and Brussels was going to take off. But the British decision to abort the Channel Tunnel sent French plans for the northern high speed line down the pan. Casting around for alternatives, SNCF planners found their eyes resting on the Atlantic seaboard.

The west was an attractive destination. It cannot have escaped government officials that better transport links in that direction would help to appease the militant population of Brittany, who in the 1960s had fomented civil disturbances which included sabotage of railway lines. At other times too the western littoral had proved to be a thorn in the flesh of French governments. The prospect of a new line to Lyons and the southeast threatened to leave western France more out on a limb than ever, so there were sound political reasons to undertake a balancing improvement in transport on the opposite side of the country.

For its part, SNCF was forecasting strong traffic growth on its main lines to the west and southwest. Mounting demand for commuter trains in the western suburbs of Paris was clogging the approach routes so that major investment seemed unavoidable in the 1990s on the lines to Tours, Le Mans and Chartres. Line capacity was already at a premium, and there seemed no way of raising it other than by adding extra tracks.

SNCF proposed a Fr3 billion package of improvements. Included was another pair of tracks in addition to the four available between Paris-Austerlitz and the junction south of Orly airport at Juvisy, one more on the three track section between Etampes and Les Aubrais outside Orléans, and an extra track between La Verrière and Le Perray on the Paris–Le Mans line. Further, the money would pay for tripling of the double track from Rambouillet to Epernon, and from Jouy to the cathedral city of Chartres. A bi-directional track would also be added between Maintenon and Chartres. But the advantages of all this would have been limited to suburban services and it was by no means clear that the effort was worthwhile.

The main lines needed attention too. Paths for *rapides* were constrained between Les Aubrais and Tours because tracks had to be shared with dilatory freights. SNCF postulated tripling or quadrupling, but as the line hugs the banks of the River Loire, this was neither a cheap nor easy option. Apart from that, extra tracks would threaten housing in Blois, midway between Orléans and Tours, as well as in four other towns.

This left the option of diverting traffic to the Paris–Tours line through Châteaudun and Vendôme, but the price of fettling it up for high speeds did not justify the limited benefits.

SNCF's planners combed the area southwest of Paris in their search for extra capacity. There they found the answer – within spitting distance of Paris Montparnasse was an abandoned railway alignment.

In 1903 a declaration of public interest had been granted to build a double track railway from Paris to Chartres via Gallardon, duplicating the route via Rambouillet. This was originally intended to provide access to Paris for the Etat Railway formed in 1878. In the event it was not until 1929 that the 70km section from Massy-Palaiseau to Chartres was completed, but this left a gap of 8km between Massy and Châtillon-sous-Bagneux.

The isolated Massy–Chartres section was worked from 1930 by a desultory *omnibus* service until 1939. Meantime, work began on the final section into Paris, reaching the boundary of the commune between Massy and Châtenay by 1935. This left a gap of 2.5km to Châtillon just outside Montparnasse; this section had been left till last because it needed tunnels under the hills at Sceaux and Fontenay-aux-Roses. The effort was too much and work was abandoned, partly because the raison d'être of the Gallardon line had been undermined by a decision in 1934 to electrify the other Paris–Chartres line, largely to relieve unemployment. During the war the Massy–Chartres line was badly damaged, and afterwards there were higher priorities than rebuilding such a backwater.

On its formation in 1937, SNCF assumed the ownership of the Gallardon alignment which had remained more or less intact. It lay forgotten, although during the 1960s various organisations sought to use the formation – it was here that Bertin built its half-scale *aérotrain* from Gometz-la-Ville to Limours. More disruptive was the construction of the Paris–Orléans/Chartres A10 motorway between Massy and Orsay. This road also breached the alignment further west between St Arnoult and Ablis.

But the crucial part of the alignment remained largely untouched until SNCF reopened the files in the 1970s. Threading the urban fabric between Fontenay-aux-Roses and Massy-Palaiseau, it offered the intriguing possibility of a high speed escape route from central Paris.

As it began just a few kilometres outside Montparnasse, it would be available for trains to accelerate to full speed only minutes after leaving the terminus – in contrast to the Paris–Sud-Est line which began 29km south of Paris-Lyons.

Between 1975 and 1977 SNCF carried out preliminary studies for a route that took in the abandoned alignment before heading southwest towards Tours and Le Mans. By mid-1977 the government of President Giscard d'Estaing was showing interest, and Minister of Supply Jean-Pierre Fourcade formally asked SNCF to initiate a feasibility study into what soon became known as *TGV-Atlantique*. SNCF estimated a route length of between 300 and 400km which would spread the benefits of high speed trains along the whole of the French Atlantic coast from the naval arsenal at Brest to the Spanish frontier.

Beyond Chartres the line would swing gently south to Châteaudun where it would bifurcate. One arm would run due west to Le Mans, the other continuing southwest towards Tours. As the main line to Bordeaux already had long stretches cleared for 200km/h, SNCF postulated a Paris–Bordeaux timing of just 3hr. Assuming electrification to Nantes and Rennes, equally dramatic journey time cuts were possible to the northwest with Brest and Quimper less than 4½hr away from the capital.

Although the Gallardon alignment helped keep costs down, there was no chance of SNCF funding TGV-Atlantique on the open market as it had with Paris–Sud-Est, and management made no secret of its anxieties. The scheme simmered on a back burner as SNCF stepped up the pace of work on the line to Lyons.

A hint of progress was given by Charles Fiterman soon after the socialist government took office in 1981 when he opened part of the A10 motorway from Poitiers to St André-de-Cubzac. The next public statement was by Mitterrand himself at the inaugural TGV dinner in Le Creusot on 22 September.

SNCF estimated the cost at Fr5 billion with a 14 per cent rate of return. The basic Y-shaped route remained, but there were refinements such as upgrading the Bordeaux main line to allow TGVs to run at 220km/h. Already the line from Le Mans to Nantes was being souped up for 200km/h as part of the 'Etoile d'Angers' electrification project which was to bring wires to all main lines radiating from Angers.

The presidential mandate gave SNCF the opening to start talks with local authorities, some of whom immediately declared themselves against the project. In mid-October the town of Blois on the Loire played host to a meeting of farmers whose land was likely to be required. With other landowners and opponents, they formed an alliance to try and block the project. A great outcry arose over the famous Vouvray vineyards, and SNCF quickly stepped in and proposed a tunnel in a bid to minimise the impact of the new line in such a sensitive area.

## Timescale for TGV-Atlantique

At this stage a preliminary timetable for construction was mooted. To allow work to begin as soon as possible after completion of the Paris–Sud-Est line the declaration of public interest would have to be granted early in the same year, meaning that public inquiries would need to be over by September 1982. That would allow tracklaying to start in 1986, with 1988 as a target date for the first Paris–Le Mans TGVs.

SNCF completed its studies in early 1982, and on 27 January the board of management assented to the proposals. The dossier was submitted to the government, which appointed Monsieur Raoul Rudeau, a noted civil engineer, to examine SNCF's findings. Rudeau's brief was to complete his investigations by the summer.

TGV-Atlantique differed from the Paris–Sud-Est TGV line in several respects. There was no need for 3.5 per cent grades as the highest relief was a paltry 200 metres. Steepest grade was set at 1.5 per cent, although this was relaxed to 2.5 per cent in seven locations. The route included four tunnels, three in the Paris suburbs, and the fourth below the Vouvray vineyards near Tours.

M Rudeau reported on 1 July 1982, concluding that the line would 'increase the mobility of large sections of the population, revive activity in sectors of the economy such as civil engineering which were in a critical state, and reinforce the strength of French industry at a time when international competition was becoming increasingly tough.'

Earthmoving. The 650 metre tunnel at Villebon-sur-Yvette on the TGV-Atlantique line in the Paris suburbs entailed moving a small hill; this enormous trench will later be filled in and landscaped. *Author*

Top level backing came on 4 November when Prime Minister Pierre Mauroy announced that the scheme would go ahead. His government recognised the 'satisfactory nature' of the plan, which was now costed at Fr12 billion, just over one third of which was for rolling stock. Six days later the Council of Ministers authorised the SNCF to take steps needed to obtain the declaration of public interest.

Although SNCF President André Chadeau welcomed the Prime Minister's decision, he reminded the government that a large financial question mark hung over the scheme. He was determined that SNCF could not afford to borrow on the open market on such a scale again, but the government did nothing to allay his concern.

Without knowing where the money was coming from, SNCF proceeded towards the public inquiry. Its inability to finance the new line lent encouragement to the antagonists, and there were suggestions that the government was going to build a political railway. Heading the opposition was a M Pierre Fauchon who was busy whipping up trouble among local authorities. The result was that when the public inquiry was launched on 25 May 1983 no less than 26 out of 33 local authorities said they would boycott it.

The inquiry made detailed documents available to the public in eight *départements*, and objections had to be submitted to M André Doumenc, a *Conseiller d'Etat* who was in charge of the inquiry at its headquarters in Chartres. When the inquiry closed on 6 July SNCF still did not know how the scheme was to be financed. On 5 August M Doumenc declared that he considered the project to be of public interest, and his report went forward to the government.

Still SNCF could not get the government to give a straight answer on funding, despite another statement from President Mitterrand during a television programme on 15 September that the second TGV line 'will be built'. Ministers had been saying this for some time, and the Ministry of Transport was obliged to clear up the confusion on the following day by issuing its own statement. It cited the cost as Fr13 billion and said that the government was prepared to contribute 30 per cent of the infrastructure bill of Fr8.4 billion; the outstanding Fr4.6 billion would pay for 91 trainsets. It only remained for the Council of State to rubber stamp the decision in May 1984.

The final alignment put the junction of the Y further southwest at Courtalain, bringing the length of the common trunk to 124km. A 52km spur would run to meet the Paris–Le Mans main line at Con-

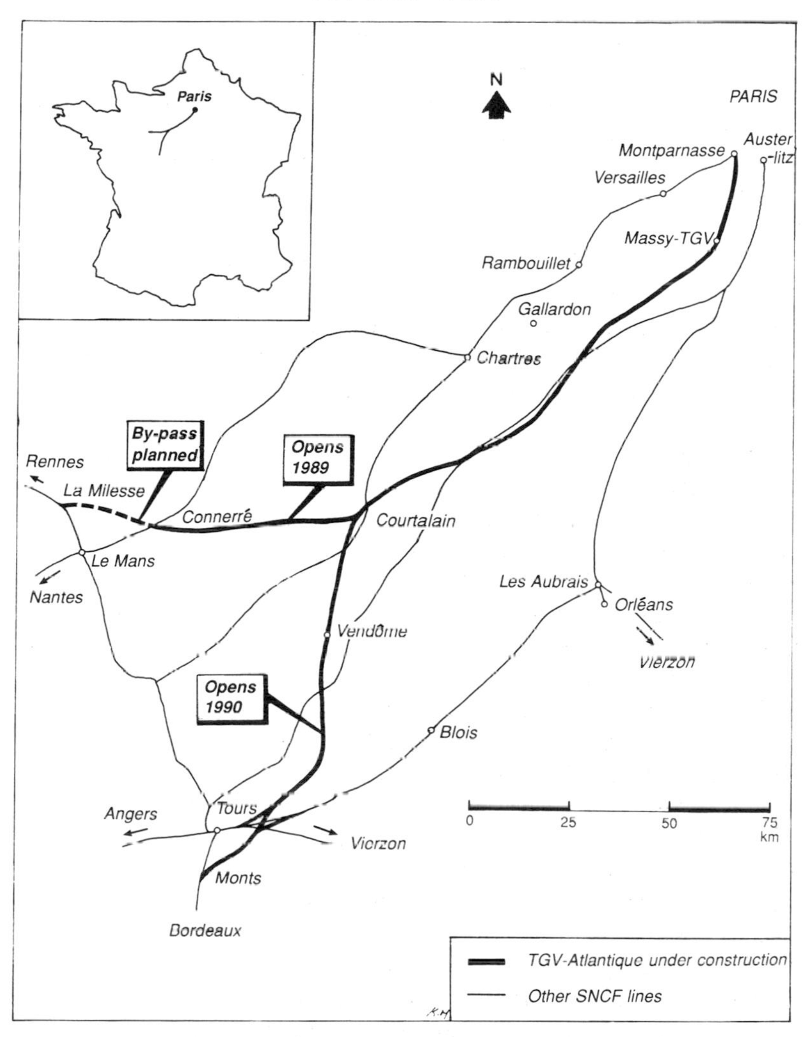


*Fig. 4.* The world's fastest railway. When France opens the TGV-Atlantique line in 1989, Nantes and Brittany will be served by trains running between Paris and Connerré at 300km/h.

nerré, while an 87km alignment would continue southwest to St Pierre des Corps outside Tours, which was to get a 17km bypass for Bordeaux bound trains. A bypass round Le Mans was postponed until an unspecified date in the future, partly because the authorities wanted all trains routed through the city. SNCF's New Line Director Étienne Chambron said in 1986 that TGVs would indeed be routed through Le Mans, but they would certainly not all stop there! The total length of new route was down to 280km.

Construction began on the Fontenay tunnel in the Paris suburbs on 7 January 1985, and an official ceremony was staged on 15 February 1985. President Mitterrand was to officiate at the somewhat remote location of the sod-turning at Boinville-le-Gaillard, 60km southwest of Paris. The site had been selected in preference to one in the Paris suburbs where feeling against the new line was running high and the political colour of some of the residents did not match that of the president. At 10.35 a helicopter landed, but out of it stepped not M Mitterrand but M Paul Quilès, who rejoiced in the title of Minister of Town Planning, Housing & Transport. The President, it turned out, was stuck in a snowdrift.

By the time work started more than 80 per cent of the land had been purchased, but the task was relatively easy as 60 per cent of the route between Paris-Montparnasse and Courtalain was either on government or SNCF owned land.

## Green corridor

Residents alongside the old Gallardon alignment through the Paris suburbs were not too happy about the prospect of TGVs rolling past their back gardens. They happened to have friends in high places, and their protests had been one of the sticking points that delayed progress with the scheme. SNCF was willing to pay for some noise suppression measures, but it was not prepared to go along with the residents' wishes for the line to be completely in tunnel.

Eventually a compromise was hammered out for a *coulée verte* or green corridor – a kind of linear park with footpaths, cycle tracks, gardens and sportsgrounds, with the government and local communities sharing the extra Fr163 million cost. Much of the line will be covered over in artificial tunnels rather like the 5.4km Pfingstberg tunnel near Mannheim in Germany. Elsewhere it will be screened by belts of trees and bushes.

In these tunnels speed will be limited to 200km/h, but once outside the suburbs the maximum will rise to 270km/h through the 4.8km Villejust tunnel (consisting of two single track bores through the Fontainebleau sands). The Vouvray tunnel which Chambron described as 'not essential but psychologically important' will be limited to 270km/h too.

The western arm is due to enter service in autumn 1989, followed a year later by the southern part of the route. In 1986 SNCF cited a Paris–Bordeaux time of 2hr 58min. Paris–Le Mans should take an even hour, with Nantes reached in 2hr 5min.

Interestingly enough, SNCF compared the TGV journey time to Bordeaux with the fastest train in the 1986 timetable which took 4hr 4min, but in 1980 both the down *Aquitaine* and the up *Etendard* Trans-Europ-Expresses were scheduled to cover the 581km between Paris Austerlitz and Bordeaux St Jean in 3hr 50min.

In 1990 20 million passengers are expected to board TGVs speeding to and from the Atlantic coast, over 4 million more than on the Paris–Sud-Est line in 1985. The higher figure is one reason why the TGV-Atlantique trainsets will have a greater capacity than their predecessors.

## Style and comfort

Several years of experience with the fleet of 109 Paris–Sud-Est TGVs gave SNCF the opportunity to evaluate the fundamental design choices of articulation and fixed formation. It saw no reason to change these for the second generation trains for TGV-Atlantique, 73 of which were ordered from Alsthom and Francorail on 24 October 1985 at a cost of Fr6.9 billion; the contract included two options, one for 10 more sets and another for 12 more.

But the traction and rolling stock engineers had not been idle. They came up with a design that promised better performance, more comfort and greater capacity while at the same time offering lower operating costs – a reconciliation of the irreconcilable, as SNCF's chief rolling stock design engineer François Lacôte put it in 1986.

Gone are the spartan seats and rather bare furnishings of the Sud-Est sets. Instead second class saloons will have fabric-covered seats and decor in swish shades of grey highlighted by turquoise and yellow. Two seating bays have been designed with families in mind with an area set aside for small children to play. This idea was introduced in the 1980s on Corail coaches.

In the first class there will be a choice of conventional open saloons and 'inglenook seating' in semi-compartments. Along one side are six seating bays, each with four seats arranged at a table; the bays are divided by partitions, with screens extending along the sides of the seats on the gangway side, giving the effect of a compartment. There are no doors, but the arrangement offers a certain amount of privacy and creates an ambience missing from the Paris–Sud-Est sets. Along the other side of the car single seats are arranged in pairs at tables.

The internal furnishings are relatively easy to change – as witnessed by the refurbishment of the bar on the Sud-Est trains. But quite fundamental changes have been made to the technical design. Partly because the TGV-Atlantique sets will have 10 instead of eight intermediate cars, the continuous rating has been raised to 4,400kW per power car.

Most significant change of all is the use of self-commutating three-phase synchronous traction motors, developed on testbed locomotive No 10004 between 1979 and 1983. This was the French riposte to the successful German asynchronous drives pioneered by Brown Boveri. Like the German Federal Railway's Class 120 locomotive, the synchronous motored No BB10004 prototype and its 'Sybic' (*Synchrone-bicourant*) derivatives have a mixed traffic capability.

During 1983 No 10004 proved equally at home hauling express passenger trains loading to, say, 650 tonnes at 200km/h and 2,000 tonne freight trains at lower speeds. SNCF believes that this capability will ultimately lead to a reduction in the size of the locomotive fleet – as one electric locomotive may cost Fr11 million, this will represent a considerable long term saving.

Synchronous motors were applied to traction in 1961 when Fernand Nouvion experimented with the idea on a 25kV electric multiple-unit in the Savoie. The technology proved somewhat ahead of its time, and operation at low speeds was far from satisfactory, leading to the experiment being abandoned. The idea was taken up again in the late 1970s when Jeumont-Schneider considered that it would be worthwhile to develop synchronous motors for railway traction, having previously built them for pumps in nuclear power stations.

A period of experimentation followed, culminating in the conversion of locomotive No 15055 to synchronous drive; after regearing for 200km/h it was renumbered 10004. It was so successful that SNCF chief engineer André Cossié said in March 1983 that SNCF was going to adopt synchronous motors for all future main line locomotive orders. Soon afterwards two more locomotives were converted as synchronous prototypes as a prelude to ordering 44 Sybic examples in mid 1984.

Thanks to the high power output possible with synchronous motors – but also because the gradients on the TGV-Atlantique line are less steep – second generation TGVs will have only four bogies powered compared with six on the original TGV design. Like their

Architect of speed. SNCF General Manager Jean Dupuy poses for the TV cameras under the digital speedometer in the bar car of synchronous-motored TGV set 10 on a demonstration trip on 23 September 1986; minutes later the speedometer showed 356 km/h. *Author*

predecessors, the TGV-Atlantique sets have a dual system capability for operating at 25kV 50Hz on the new line and at 1.5kV dc on existing routes. In fact, the section of new line round Tours will be electrified at 1.5kV dc and fed by a substation at Larcay. This is because SNCF wants to use the Tours bypass for locomotive-hauled passenger and freight trains which do not need to call at Tours or St-Pierre-des-Corps.

On 23 September 1986 SNCF staged a TGV demonstration run from Paris to Le Creusot and back. On board was a large contingent of media and a goodly selection of chief executives from Europe's rolling stock suppliers, including Britain's Brush and GEC. SNCF was particularly keen to show off this particular TGV set, for it was the prototype for TGV-Atlantique. It boasted new air suspension bogies which improved significantly on the earlier design and synchronous three-phase traction motors.

The trip had been carefully timed to follow the ICE demonstration towards the end of September – although officially it was pure coincidence. As it happened the French had no need to worry about their world record because of the ICE derailment – which immediately halted all the chat in Frankfurt about 400km/h. All the same, the French have a knack of doing things with panache. At Le Creusot some elaborate full-size mock-ups of the interior of the next generation of trains were on display. General Manager Jean Dupuy hinted in a speech that the return journey would include some high speed running to give a foretaste of what it would be like to ride on TGV-Atlantique.

The trip turned out to be a publicity stunt which found Dupuy posing for the TV crews under a digital speedometer in the bar car. Above his head the figures flickered past 300, climbing steadily to culminate at a dramatic 356km/h. So it is that the French and not the Germans hold the world record for three-phase traction. The speed of 356km/h also happened to be 1km/h more than the magnetically-levitated Transrapid 06 had reached in December 1985. Most significant of all, the trip demonstrated that the French have mastered the technology to run at 300km/h – the speed at which TGV-Atlantique services will operate on the day the line opens in 1989.

# 11
# SHINKANSEN BOUNCES BACK

While DB was struggling to meet the demands of lineside residents and come to terms with the strident calls of environmentalists campaigning against new lines, JNR was on the receiving end of a hail of similar protests. The Narita airport route was to all intents and purposes abandoned, and priority had switched to the two northern shinkansen because of their potential to stimulate economic growth and tourism.

The Sapporo shinkansen had been cut back to the 496km from Tokyo to Morioka, and this route became known as the Tohoku shinkansen. This was being built in parallel with the 270km Joetsu shinkansen from Omiya, a junction about 30km outside Tokyo on the Tohoku line, to Niigata. Both lines had been affected by the problem of noise. This had inflated costs because of the need to construct all kinds of sound absorbing structures.

A range of noise suppression techniques had been tried out on a 43km test section of the Tohoku line between Kukishi and Ishibashimachi built in advance of the rest of the route; one of the most effective methods was to erect inverted L shaped parapets alongside the track; these trap the noise generated by running gear and also form walkways for staff. The extra work meant that by 1977 construction of both routes was badly behind schedule, and talk of further expansion or higher speeds was out of the question.

The area served by the Tohoku line alone is home to 35 million people. In contrast, the Joetsu line traverses a sparsely populated but beautiful area with considerable tourist potential. It pierces the heart of the Mikumi mountain range in the 22.2km Daishimizu tunnel between Jomokogen and Echigo Yuzawa. Until the Seikan tunnel under the Tsugaru straits between Honshu and Hokkaido opens in 1988, this remains the world's longest rail tunnel.

The Daishimizu was a massive job, but not as it turned out the most difficult. Worse problems were encountered with the 14.8 Nakayama tunnel between Takasaki and Jomokogen. Construction workers had a nasty surprise when the volcanic rocks in which they were working began to gush torrents of water under high pressure, flooding uncontrollably into the workings. The line was being built by Japan Railway Construction Corporation, a company formed in 1964 to construct new railways with financial help from the government. JRCC had to resort to chemical grouting, adding further delay.

North of Jomokogen the Joetsu line runs through an area where snow often piles up to a depth of 4 metres. On the highest parts of the route snowsheds protect the track from heavy snow and avalanches, while in open country hot water sprays melt the snow before it builds up.

The Joetsu line required the most extensive civil engineering of any shinkansen, with 106km or 39 per cent in tunnel. It was partly to save money that it was combined with the Tohoku line over the last section into Tokyo; originally it was to terminate at Shinjuku station in the west of the city.

But access to Tokyo was the most difficult problem of all. Only in November 1978 did JNR even reach agreement with local government for the route over the crucial section through the suburbs from Omiya to central Tokyo. As part of the bargain, JNR undertook to widen the shinkansen viaduct structures to accept an automated peoplemover providing local transport for lineside residents who would otherwise watch the shinkansen trains streaking past with no tangible advantages to themselves.

Construction of the Omiya–Tokyo section did not start until 25 June 1980, and even then local residents still had legal action pending in the courts. Not only that, but the terminus was not to be Tokyo main station – JNR had been forced to settle on Ueno to the north of the city centre, as the problem of building through the heart of the capital was even more intractable than trying to penetrate the suburbs.

## Tohoku and Joetsu lines open

The Tohoku was the first of the two lines to open. A preliminary service of 10 trains a day each way began running at 210km/h on 23 June 1982. Less than five months later, on 15 November, the service was trebled. On the same day JNR President Fumio Takagi inaugurated the Joetsu line at a ceremony in Niigata on the Sea of Japan coast. There were 21 trains a day in each direction.

Mirroring the Tokaido–Sanyo service pattern, the northern shinkansen have two types of train. The equivalent of the fast *Hikari* is the *Yamabiko* (mountain echo) on the Tohoku route and *Asahi* (morning sun) on the Joetsu. All-stops services are *Aoba* (green leaves) and *Toki* (crested ibis) respectively. JNR chose the names from thousands suggested by 150,000 people in a competition in 1981.

Traffic was not all it might have been as neither Tohoku or Joetsu trains actually ran into Tokyo. Their temporary terminus at Omiya was well outside the city, a considerable disincentive for business travel. The gap was bridged by 1,067mm gauge shuttle trains which ferried passengers to and from Ueno. Here massive reconstruction was needed to accommodate the shinkansen – when it eventually got there. Ueno was already a two-level station with through tracks on elevated structures and terminating tracks below, and space for the four shinkansen tracks could only be found several floors below ground.

Once construction of the Omiya-Ueno section began in 1980, work progressed rapidly. In May 1984 JNR announced that through shinkansen services from Ueno to Niigata and Morioka would start in March 1985.

Opening of the Tohoku and Joetsu routes with all their anti-noise measures did not provoke the howls of protest that JNR had feared, and JNR began to contemplate a speed-up.

Perhaps more crucial than any other single factor was a ruling on 11 September 1980 by the Nagoya district court that saved Tokaido shinkansen trains from the fate of being forced to run at less than a third of their 210km/h design speed over a 7km stretch through the city. Even though JNR had to shell out ¥530 million for 'psychological damage' inflicted on lineside dwellers, Judge Kohei Kachi's decision effectively meant that slowing down the shinkansen would bring greater social hardship to the nation, and that if the trains were to be decelerated in Nagoya they would logically have to run slower elsewhere too – thereby destroying the raison d'être of the whole shinkansen.

Soon after the Nagoya ruling a 110km/h speed restriction was lifted on the final section of the Sanyo shinkansen in Kyushu – it had been in force ever since the line had opened in 1975.

JNR was encouraged. Times had been hard – apart from the noise battles, JNR's finances had been running out of control, largely as a result of government policy. Drastic attempts to put JNR on solid

High-rise track. Joetsu shinkansen train near Yuzawa cruises on structures that dwarf surrounding houses; the size of the viaduct is exaggerated by the sound barrier walls enclosing the track. *Japan National Tourist Organization*

High-rise train. Double-deck cars are a popular feature of the Series 100 trains on the Tokaido shinkansen. Similar trains are now being built for the Tohoku route.

financial ground had all failed, and JNR had been obliged to make swingeing fares increases, leading to a drop in traffic. This had been serious enough for some Tokaido shinkansen services to be cut in October 1979, with *Kodama* services shortened from 16 to 12 cars. The Nagoya ruling was a watershed that restored confidence, coming as it did hard on the heels of JNR winning its fight to build the Omiya–Ueno section.

There was certainly scope for a speed-up on the Tohoku shinkansen, which like the Sanyo had been designed with 260km/h in mind. It was a question of whether to push for the full 260km/h or to settle for something less ambitious.

## Rolling stock replacement

When new rolling stock was needed for the Sanyo extension to Okayama and Hakata, JNR examined the prospects for a new generation of trains that might run at 260km/h. To try out new techniques such as aluminium bodywork and thyristor control, JNR had a two-car Series 951 prototype built in 1969. It was geared to run at 275km/h, and among other innovations it boasted frictionless eddy-current brakes.

During trials Series 951 was coaxed up to 286km/h, but the unit demonstrated that moving up from 210 to 260km/h was not as easy as it appeared. Apart from anything else the eddy-current rail brakes, although effective, had the unfortunate side effect of heating up the rails – the same problem that the French had encountered with Zébulon.

Compatibility with existing Tokaido line stock won the day, and the new stock was almost identical to the original design. Minor changes included smaller windows to minimise the chances of them being shattered by flying ballast.

Even when it came to replacing the original stock, there seemed no point in choosing a different design. Replacements were needed not long after the Sanyo line opened. After a dozen years of pounding up and down the world's busiest inter-city rail corridor, the original trains were simply worn out. In 1976 the first of a series of 360 replacement cars ordered at the end of 1975 was delivered. So began a rolling replacement programme which continued with the same design of train into the mid-1980s.

Compatibility was not a problem for the northern shinkansen rolling stock as the lines were physically isolated from the Tokaido–

Sanyo line; the power supply was also different, being 25kV 50Hz north of Tokyo and 25kV 60Hz on the earlier lines. (This is because Japan has two national grids, 60Hz south of Tokyo and 50Hz in the north.) So JNR chose to develop a different design reflecting recent advances in traction techniques and able to run at 260km/h.

## Prototype sets

The first Joetsu/Tohoku prototype was the thyristor-controlled six-car Series 961 which emerged in 1973. The weight of more powerful electrical equipment needed for 260km/h running was compensated by the light alloy bodywork and improvements in power semiconductors, insulation and cooling equipment. Other changes included a new bogie design and a variety of novel internal layouts.

In 1977 a second six-car prototype was ordered. By this time opposition to the shinkansen was mounting sharply, and JNR temporarily abandoned hopes of 260km/h. Thus Series 962 had motors rated at only 230kW compared with 275kW on the 961. Provision for automatic train operation was also dropped.

The 962 was delivered in 1979, and JNR began a series of high speed trials with the two trains. The 961 was whipped up to 292km/h on 28 November, with 304km/h being attained two days later. On 7 December the test crew worked their steed up to 319km/h, a shinkansen record. The trials were completed in the following month, and JNR announced on 20 January – prematurely as it happened – that the speed on the northern shinkansen would be 260km/h.

Then came the cuts on the Tokaido line, and with more delays becoming inevitable on the northern shinkansen construction schedules, JNR decided that discretion might after all be the better part of valour. No more was heard about speed increases until the Nagoya court ruling induced a more favourable attitude towards high speed running among the public and with the government.

JNR then went ahead and ordered 432 cars of seven different types for the two northern routes. The first of these Series 200 cars was moved by sea from the Kawasaki plant in Kobe to Niigata towards the end of 1980. It could not travel by rail as there was no standard gauge connection across Tokyo – even if the section from Omiya to Ueno had been completed.

The 12 car Series 200 formation has one green car and a buffet coach and is distinguished from the Series 0 trains on the Tokaido–

Sanyo line by a green instead of a blue band along the windows. Externally, there are few differences, but the new trains embodied the lessons that had been learnt with the various prototypes; for example they included thyristor control of the traction motor power supply and chopper control of dynamic braking.

The whole design was geared to combat the snow: underfloor equipment was fully enclosed, and below the bullet nose was a snow-plough that flung the powder into lineside recesses. Air inlets on each car led into centrifugal separators to ensure snow could not penetrate passenger compartments or sensitive electrical apparatus. Great efforts were made to reduce noise from its sources at the wheel/rail interface and on the pantograph.

In the meantime JNR was undertaking massive renewal work on the Tokaido line to keep it in tip-top condition – not an easy task when faced with intensive use and only the nightly 6hr window available for track and catenary maintenance. Reliability on the route had peaked after teething troubles had been ironed out, with high standards of punctuality and service achieved up to 1971. From then onwards, with more and more trains being run, problems that might have been easily dealt with earlier assumed greater significance.

Faults in the automatic train control equipment had caused serious alarm on a number of occasions; once instruments had given a clear reading for a driver to proceed at 210km/h when in fact the train was supposed to be halted in a station. Nevertheless, the line had carried undreamt of quantities of passengers, and not one of them had been killed or injured by any fault of JNR. The shinkansen had made a staggering profit and astounded the world. JNR had no choice but to rebuild.

Renewal with 60kg/m rail instead of the original 53kg/m began in 1972. Particularly difficult to fit in was the relaying of pointwork. So it was that JNR instituted what was to become a regular feature – for about eight mornings a year the shinkansen was closed to all traffic to give the maintenance teams a clear 12hr stretch.

Replacement of overhead line equipment was also necessary. Wire with a heavier cross-section strung at a higher tension was substituted as it was less vulnerable to high winds; its greater stiffness also gave pantographs at the rear of the train a better chance of following the vertical oscillations of the contact wire set up by the leading pantographs.

Yet rebuilding was not enough. Road and air competition – particularly with wide-bodied jets flying shuttle services – was nibbling away at JNR's prime market. JNR was keen to see its money-spinning line continue to make a profit, so it instigated a review of high speed potential in 1983.

Tests were carried out with a Series 925–S2 car (which had the same mechanical design as Series 200) in 1983–84 to assess the possibilities of 240km/h on the Tohoku line. Later it was run at 260km/h.

Trials conducted in 1979–80 with Series 0 cars at the same time as JNR was testing the Series 961 had shown that it would be feasible to run at 220 or 230km/h on the original Tokaido line without too much extra expense. These studies were re-examined in 1983–84, and more tests followed at 220km/h on various parts of the Tokaido line. But JNR was not quite ready for a major Tokaido line speed-up, although as a prelude it did shave 2min off the fastest Tokyo–Osaka timings in March 1985 to give a 3hr 8min journey – an average speed of 164.5km/h.

### Ueno link opens

March 1985 was a crucial month. On 14 March JNR finally opened the 27.5km Omiya–Ueno shinkansen link; *Yamabiko* 31 was the first train to leave Ueno for Morioka at 06.00 in a ceremony attended by JNR President Iwao Nisugi and Transport Minister Yamashita. First arrival at Ueno was at 08.22 from Sendai, followed at 08.34 by *Asahi* 390 from Niigata on the Joetsu line. The number of Tohoku line daily round trips was stepped up from 30 to 47, and from 21 to 34 on the Joetsu route. On the previous day two new stations on the Tohoku shinkansen had been opened at Mizusawa Esashi and Shin Hanamaki, but the really significant event on 14 March was raising of the speed of selected Tohoku line trains from 210 to 240km/h.

Taken together with the Ueno opening, this cut the fastest Tokyo Ueno–Morioka time from 3 hr 56min to 2hr 45min. The Tokyo Ueno–Niigata time came down from 2hr 33min to 1hr 53min. Within weeks traffic began to soar up. After a month airline traffic on the Tohoku route had plummetted by 60 per cent, and Toa Domestic Airlines withdrew its twice-daily Tokyo–Hanamaki flight (Hanamaki is just south of the Tohoku line terminus at Morioka).

Then, on 26 March, JNR unveiled the prototype of the third generation shinkansen train, Series 100. Distinguished by a long drooping nose with a better aerodynamic performance than earlier designs, the Series 100 was JNR's bid to bring a touch of luxury to the bullet trains that might woo traffic back from the airlines – in 1984 JNR had 29 per cent of the Tokyo–Fukuoka (Hakata) market while the airlines had 71 per cent. So the new train was given a unique attraction – a pair of double-deck cars marshalled in the centre of the formation; each carries a red symbol signifying New Shinkansen.

The prototype began running trials in April, and by August it had reached 230km/h on the Tokaido line and 260km/h on the Sanyo line. It entered revenue service in October 1985 and was an immediate hit with the public. JNR was so encouraged that it brought forward plans for a production version, ordering the first batch in autumn 1985. The first five sets had entered service by November 1986, when they worked four *Hikari* round trips a day between Tokyo and Hakata.

On 1 November JNR raised maximum speed on the Tokaido line from 210 to 220km/h, with the Series 100 trains working the fastest schedules thanks to their superior acceleration of 1.6 metres/sec$^2$. They cover the 1,069km between Tokyo and Hakata in 5h 57min, an average of 179.7km/h including six stops. After 22 years the original goal of bringing Osaka within 3hr of Tokyo was also realised with a timing of 2hr 58min.

Each Series 100 set offers 1,153 standard class seats and 112 in the green cars. The green car accommodation is split between one double-deck and one single-deck car. On the lower deck of the double-decker are nine compartments: five for one person, three for two and one for three. They are ideal for businessmen wishing to work or for anyone seeking privacy, although they do command a hefty supplement.

The second double-decker is a diner, with a 44 seat restaurant on the top deck served from a kitchen below. Panoramic curved windows with sun-dim glass offer an excellent view – they are larger on the production cars than on the prototype. JNR found that the upper deck restaurant was exceptionally popular, as was the upper deck of the green car. Not that you have to go to the diner on the shinkansen – there is a constant procession of food vendors plying up and down the train; Japanese etiquette requires them to bow to the passengers when they enter or leave the green car.

JNR had reason to be well pleased with its new design. Apart from its instant acceptance by customers it had its own attraction for the operator. Compared with Series 0, it offered energy savings of around 17 per cent thanks to better aerodynamics and lower weight resulting from less traction equipment – neither the double-deckers nor the end driving cars are powered. The axleload is also reduced from 16 to 15 tonnes, and interior noise levels are 3db(A) lower than on Series 0.

Having previously discarded eddy-current rail brakes, JNR experimented on the prototype Series 100 with friction-free eddy-current disc brakes mounted on the axles. These had been tried on the Series 925 track inspection train, but not in intensive service, so extra testing was carried out in the laboratory. They worked sufficiently well to warrant their installation on the production build, but only after a year or two will JNR have enough experience to judge whether they are an economic proposition. The heat build-up is considerable, but JNR says it has found a material that can stop the temperature rising about 150°C; the disc life is largely dependent on how efficiently heat is dissipated.

## Fourth generation planned

Partly because of noise and vibration problems, but also because of the high aerodynamic drag in tunnels, existing shinkansen trains cannot run at more than about 270km/h in commercial service. To go beyond that requires major design changes which the Japanese rolling stock builders began to investigate while the prototype Series 100 was under construction.

By the end of 1986 JNR had defined the fundamental design characteristics and drawn up tentative plans for construction of a prototype by 1989. An important change was the adoption of a smaller cross-section to cut aerodynamic drag, giving a profile not far removed from the French TGV. The problem is that a narrower cross-section may limit seating to 2+2 instead of 2+3. This would almost certainly be unacceptable on the Tokaido line where standing is common in the non-reserved cars. It would however suffice for other routes with lower traffic density.

Traction equipment with three-phase drives and gate turn-off thyristors in the main power control circuits would be designed to give a maximum speed of 300km/h – from whence comes the designation of Series 300. Bolsterless bogies and lightweight aluminium construction giving an axleload of around 14 tonnes are envisaged. But the exact shape and characteristics of the 'Super Hikari' Series 300 could not be decided by JNR. For JNR ceased to exist on 1 April 1987.

For years JNR had been saddled with a cumulative debt burden that amounted to squillions of yen – sums so large as to be meaningless, although the *Financial Times* put it rather well on December 12 1986 by pointing out the long-term liabilities amounted to more than the debts of Brazil and Mexico together. Practically all this consists of interest payments needed to service earlier debts.

Since the 1960s the Japanese government made several attempts to bring the runaway finances under control, all of them meeting with no success, largely because of the equivocal requirement for JNR to manage a tight financial ship without having the freedom to charge market prices. The government always insisted on having the last word on fares – and wages. On top of that JNR found itself paying pensions to more people than it actually employed – and it employed far more people than were actually necessary to run the railway. Their forced removal to other jobs was quite a revolution in a country where the firm you work for normally guarantees a job for life.

All this had got so out of hand by 1983 that the subject had become a major political issue. Prime Minister Yasushiro Nakasone was elected partly on a ticket that said he was going to cure JNR's financial ills once and for all. His choice of method was drastic in the extreme – carve JNR up into seven regional companies, six passenger and one freight, with the ultimate intention of turning them over to the private sector. An advisory panel was set up to report on the idea, which ran into considerable opposition in JNR – even at the highest level.

When it became obvious in 1985 that even the top brass were willing to fight the proposals of the government's advisory panel, Nakasone called in JNR President Iwao Nisugi – appointed by Nakasone in 1983 – to tell him that no compromise would be possible. Nisugi promptly resigned, to be followed on the next day by his vice president and chief engineer. This episode prompted the *Japan Times* to describe Nakasone's behaviour as a 'reign of terror'.

With almost headstrong determination, Nakasone had by the end of 1986 pushed through the Diet a series of bills establishing the JNR reform which took effect on 1 April 1987. Since then the national railways have been known as the Japan Rail (JR) Group.

Under the legislation, a shinkansen holding company owns all infrastructure and equipment except rolling stock. This leases the infrastructure to the regional passenger railway companies – which were established on a geographical basis. This gives the following structure: Tohoku and Joetsu shinkansen operated by the East Japan Passenger Railway Co, the Tokaido shinkansen run by the Tokai Passenger Railway Co and the Sanyo shinkansen operated by the West Japan Passenger Railway Co.

## Network expansion

While the threat of the JNR break-up turned from political ideology to harsh reality the government continued to pursue plans for expansion of the shinkansen network. There was tremendous political pressure to extend the benefits of high speed trains to cities well off the shinkansen map. In the mid-1980s the nationwide shinkansen once again came under discussion, with five lines having priority:

- the Tohoku line extension from Morioka to Aomori (175km);
- the Hokuriku line from Takasaki on the Joetsu line to Osaka via the Sea of Japan coast (600km);
- the Kyushu line from Hakata to Nishi Kagoshima (249km);
- a second line on Kyushu from Hakata to Nagasaki (125km);
- the Hokkaido line from Hakodate to Sapporo 225km).

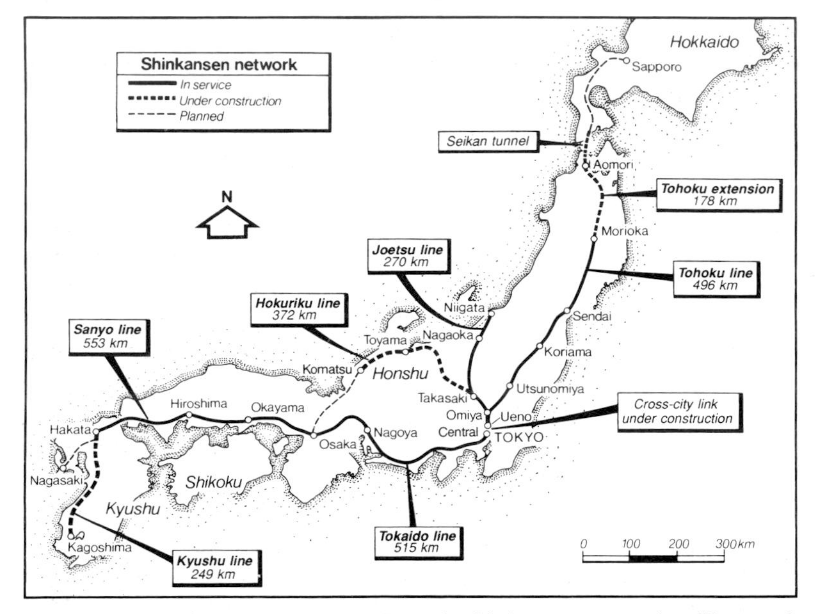


*Fig 5.* By the end of the century Japan's shinkansen network will extend from Hokkaido to Kyushu. *Railway Gazette International.*

JNR was encouraged to plan ahead for these lines, even though the cabinet had imposed a ban on construction of new shinkansen lines in September 1982 because of JNR's financial ills. This was formally lifted early in 1987, clearing one of many obstacles from the path leading to a restart. First on the list was the Morioka–Aomori extension of the Tohoku line, and construction of Shin Aomori station, 3.8km from central Aomori, had actually begun on 18 December 1985. This was not quite the same as proper construction of the new line – a truly enormous job because two thirds of the route is in tunnel. The ¥640 billion scheme includes the 26.5km Hokkoda tunnel and another bore of 25.8km at Iwate.

The Aomori extension forms the first stage of the shinkansen link to Hokkaido through the 53.8km Seikan tunnel under the Tsugaru straits. Plans for the tunnel existed as long ago as the 1930s, but the proposals gained considerable momentum after 1,430 people drowned in September 1954 when the *Toyamaru* ferry and other ships sank in a typhoon. The exceptionally difficult geology of the strata under the straits meant that it took 14 years for the main tunnels to be holed through, and the first Seikan tunnel services will run in March 1988. They will be ordinary 1,067mm gauge trains until the shinkansen is further extended from Aomori to the tunnel portal, allowing high speed trains to reach Hakodate on Hokkaido. The Hakodate–Sapporo shinkansen when it is eventually finished will put Sapporo only 5hr 40min away from Tokyo.

But other shinkansen routes may be finished before that. In early 1986 the Japan Railway Construction Corporation sought approval from the Ministry of Transport to start work on the 372km section of the Hokuriku shinkansen from Takasaki to Toyama and Komatsu. Piercing Japan's central mountain range, it will have 47 per cent of the route in tunnel; construction of the Iiyama tunnel, the longest on the line, began during 1986. The route has 11 intermediate stations and is designed for 260km/h, even though it may well be worked by Series 300 trains capable of 300km/h. Journey time for the 475km from Tokyo to Komatsu will be 3hr compared with about 4½hr using the Tokaido shinkansen to Maibara and changing there to the 1,067mm gauge Hokuriku line. The present journey to Toyama takes about 6hr, and this will be pared to 2½hr with the new line.

Outlying Kyushu was the next location to merit a symbolic start on a shinkansen. A government committee agreed on 1 December 1986 to permit work to go ahead on the 275km Kyushu line, and sod-turning ceremonies were staged only a week later in Kagoshima and Kumamoto. This route will connect end-on at Hakata with the Sanyo line, and services will be worked by six-car trains running at 260km/h, taking 90min to reach Nishi Kagoshima with eight stops en route. Excluding the cost of the trains, this line has a price tag of ¥868 billion.

On 25 August 1986 the Transport Ministry announced that work would restart in 1987 on the 3.6km link between Tokyo Central and Ueno across the heart of the city. This will allow Tohoku and Joetsu line passengers to interchange directly to the Tokaido line. Work had begun in 1981 but was halted in 1983. Costing 10 times as much per

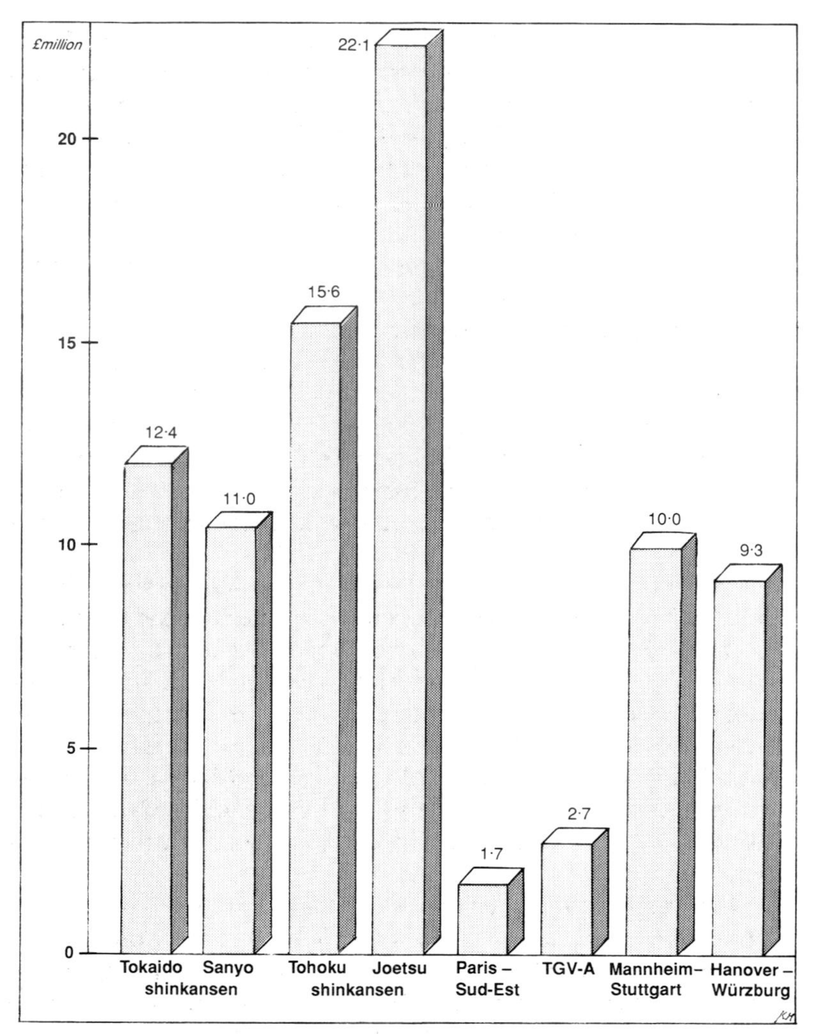


*Fig 6.* Construction cost per km of high speed lines in Japan, France and West Germany in £million at 1984 values. The cost of the Joetsu line is explained by the tunnels and viaducts needed to cross Japan's central mountain range; the relative cost of the Paris–Sud-Est line, which has no tunnels, is minimal.

km as the other lines now planned, it entails a steep grade in tunnel from the depths of Ueno station to a section on viaduct parallel to JNR's existing cross-city suburban lines. Completion is due in 1989.

Ways of reducing construction costs on the new lines have been the subject of much heated discussion within the various government committees which have the job of sorting out what will actually be built. The possibility of TGV style up-and-over construction was canvassed, but the Japanese mountains are formidable terrain compared with the gently rolling hills of central France. Savings are more likely to come from smaller structures – possible with modern materials – from less elaborate stations with two instead of four tracks, and developments in tunnelling technology.

Even so, the cost of building the lines is astronomical. In mid-1986 JNR was citing a price of between ¥3 and ¥4 billion per km (1984 prices), in real terms about the same as the first part of the Sanyo line and still below the cost of the Joetsu route which was over ¥7 billion per km (also 1984 value). JNR quoted a total bill for the five new lines of over ¥5,000 billion, but at the end of that year it revised the cost upwards to more than ¥7,000 billion. On the assumption that the lines open in 1993, they would turn in an overall profit in 1996–97, although the Hokkaido line and the route to Nagasaki would run at a loss.

A more radical suggestion to save money is to lay a third or fourth rail along 1,067mm gauge lines, something which would have to be accompanied by massive upgrading and realignment, but which would still be much cheaper than full-blown new construction. This would allow shinkansen trains to run beyond the high speed lines in the same way as French TGVs reach Grenoble, Lyon, Montpellier, Marseilles and Nice. Another idea put forward by the East Japan Passenger Railway Co is for a dual-gauge Talgo design able to run at 200km/h on the shinkansen and 160km/h on the 1,067mm gauge network.

JNR thought dual-gauge would only be possible on one or two routes such as Sendai to Yamagata, but it seems that all kinds of political problems have been thrown up by this suggestion. Legally the upgraded routes would not be classed as shinkansen, necessitating a new funding structure in which the government would like to see local authorities participate. Although they are keen to reap the benefits of high speed inter-city trains, they are not quite so keen to delve in their pockets to get them. Whether the idea will ever be taken further will only be known once the JR Group has bedded down.

# 12

# ROME REVIVES THE DIRETTISSIMA

After the TGV stormed past the British HST in 1981, France and Japan remained the uncontested leaders in the high speed league table. Suddenly, in 1985, a new competitor appeared. Italy's entry was somewhat unexpected, as the ambitious plans for new lines and rolling stock which its State Railways had cherished during the 1970s had all but stagnated.

The high speed aspirations of the Italian Railway authority (FS) date back to the inter-war period – a high speed line termed a *direttissima* had been completed in 1927 from Rome to Naples, but the term had been coined as early as 1914 when work had first started. A second *direttissima* entailing construction of 30 tunnels, one of them 18.5km long, was completed in 1934 from Bologna through the Apennine mountains to Prato (for Florence).

It was on the Rome – Naples *direttissima* that an ETR201 three car electric trainset logged a speed of slightly more than 200km/h on a special run in June 1938. Even more spectacular was a trip just over a year later with the same trainset that shot over the 314km from Florence to Milan at a staggering average speed of nearly 164km/h, reaching a peak of 203km/h. A 6hr timing between Milan and Rome was briefly attained by service trains in the same year, but war and the ensuing havoc put paid to further high speed running until the 1950s.

In 1953 the legendary seven-car luxury *Settebello* trainsets with full-width forward observation lounges at each end and a driver's cab perched in a cupola on top of the lounge reintroduced the 6hr schedule on the prime route from Milan to Rome. After that FS made strenuous efforts to accelerate main line services, and a family of streamlined railcars designated Ale601 was commissioned; they worked mainly on long distance runs such as the Rome–Palermo *Pel-*

*oritano*. Some of these cars were geared for 180km/h, and one clocked 250km/h on the Rome–Naples *direttissima* in 1968.

By this time the shinkansen had been operating at 210km/h for four years, a fact that had escaped neither the FS management nor the Italian government. Italy's north–south trunk lines were congested and slow, and in 1969 the government and the railways announced bold plans to build Europe's first shinkansen between Rome and Florence. Today the term *direttissima* generally refers to this project.

Italians adore the grand style. The spectacularly huge glass and concrete cathedral called Rome Termini that squats in front of the Piazza dei Cinquecento typifies this instinct to impress. The Rome–Florence *direttissima* was cast in the same mould, but its grandiose style made it a megaproject that absorbed so many billions of lira that it nearly became a useless monument to the engineers who conceived it. Fortunately the ingenuity of Italy's rolling stock designers is about to rescue it from such an ignominious fate.

Due to enter service in 1988 is a fleet of high performance 3kV dc trains able to run on the *direttissima* at 250km/h, and these are but the forerunners of a generation of trains that FS believes will rival the TGV. They would never have been built had it not been for Fiat's Y-0160 high speed tilting test car constructed in 1972 and its successor the *Pendolino* (Chapter 4).

The *direttissima* as first conceived in 1968 entailed building four cut-offs totalling 120km and reconstructing the rest of the old Rome–Florence line that had been completed as a double track artery in the 1930s. The entire route was designed for 250km/h and all the work was to be completed within five years.

One of the difficulties of upgrading the old route on such a scale was the inevitable massive disruption to traffic, which FS quickly decided was not permissible. It revised the plans and came up with a project that extended new construction to more than 90 per cent of the route, cutting 80km off the 316km over the old line between the two cities.

Like DB, FS had chosen to build its new line for passenger and freight trains, dictating huge radius curves and shallow gradients. Another fundamental principle was that the new route would have links to the old line at several locations, adding another 53km of new construction. These 'interconnections' permitted trains to be switched on and off the new line to serve intermediate stations or branches such as the Ancona route diverging at Orte. The effect was to create a four track trunk artery on which freight and passenger trains could easily be switched out of each other's paths.

This was of particular significance for Italy's seasonal peak traffic flows when there is sudden demand for line capacity. At the time of the citrus fruit harvest, for example, thousands of tonnes of lemons and oranges have to be whisked to markets north of the Alps in double quick time. Summer holiday traffic saturates the trunk lines in the same way, while the phenomenon of frequent elections brings its own special problems as thousands of Italians working in Switzerland and Germany travel home to vote.

## *Direttissima* construction

A law passed by the Italian parliament in October 1968 freed 200 billion lire for *direttissima* work to go ahead, but money values sank in 1969 with alarming rapidity, so that instead of letting contracts for the whole 236km it was only possible to fund 142km. But even this cutback was not enough, and a further 100 billion lire had to be obtained from the government for civil engineering work, with another 12 billion for signalling. With 312 billion available, contractors began work on four lots in early 1970.

FS concentrated on the Tiber valley section immediately north of Rome from the junction with the old line at Settebagni (16km from Rome Termini) to Città della Pieve, 122km on the new route towards Florence. This section included 42km of tunnel and one of the world's longest railway viaducts, the 5.4km crossing of the Paglia valley. During the early construction phase this huge structure was a mecca for visitors excited by the prospect of a European shinkansen.

The International Union of Railways for instance chose the *direttissima* as an example of progress with Europe's future high speed lines and ran at least two lavish press trips for European transport correspondents to view the work. One was in November 1973 when the last of 205 gigantic 25 metre box beam spans weighing 250 tonnes was lowered ceremonially into position on the Paglia viaduct.

This event was followed by a copious lunch in a nearby *castiglio*, after which guests were bustled into a special train back to Rome to connect with that evening's *Palatino* sleeping car service to Paris. No sooner had they boarded the special, which was running late because lunch had taken far too long, than the guests were offered further refreshment. Back in Rome, the press staggered across to the *Palatino* in the 10min remaining before departure. As soon as it left, the wretched correspondents were invited to take their seats in the Wagons-Lits restaurant car . . .

The sort of ballyhoo being made of the *direttissima* began to look a little sick by 1975, when the opening date was set for the Settebagni–Città delle Pieve section. There had already been suggestions that construction should be halted because of rising costs and failure to agree on the route at several locations. An over-run of more that 50 billion lire on the first tranche with its 16 tunnels totalling 41km aroused accusations of bungling, and another 200 billion lire had to be obtained in 1975. In the meantime a start on the final section into Florence was heavily delayed because of a dispute over the alignment through the suburbs.

1975 came and went, and no opening took place. It was not until 16 September 1976 that trains ran over the Orvieto–Città della Pieve section, followed on 14 December by commissioning of the Settebagni–Gallese sector. The official inauguration ceremony was delayed until 14 February 1977 when the Orte–Orvieto part of the route opened.

Even then the 122km was split in two by an uncompleted tunnel at Orte where layers of sand interspersed in the pliocene clay had presented the tunnellers with unforeseen problems. These were compounded by the discovery of high pressure springs which poured a river of mud into the workings, putting back completion until April 1980. It was in any case an exceptionally complicated tunnelling job as it included an underground junction with the old line; because of the delay a temporary connection had to be laid south of the tunnel.

Construction of the northern tip of the line into Florence ran into similar trouble where the San Donato tunnel – nearly 11km in length – revealed another unsuspected set of strata, polishing off any hopes of opening anywhere near the original schedule.

When the first *rapidi* were diverted off the old route in 1976 the gain in time from running on the new alignment was minimal as FS possessed no rolling stock (apart from the *Pendolino*) able to attain the line's design speed of 250km/h. Nor was the signalling on the new line fit for high speed operation, with the result that maximum speed was held down to 160km/h.

The powerful Bo-Bo Class E444 locomotives were rendered partially impotent by the refusal of the civil engineers to sanction them to run at their design speed of 200km/h because of fears that they would exert dynamic overloads on the track. This gave a bitter twist to the wry FS humour of calling the E444 the Tortoise class – each locomotive has a picture of a speeding tortoise emblazoned on the cab sides. The tortoises were banned from exceeding 180km/h.

Plans for a souped-up Co-Co version called the E666 progressed no

Grand designs. Italian State Railways 'Tortoise' Class E444 locomotive thunders across the Paglia viaduct on the Rome–Florence *direttissima*; although the Trans-Europ-Express coaches can run at 200km/h, most E444 locomotives are limited to 180km/h. *FS*

Son of Pendolino. The first bodyshell of the Fiat built 250 km/h ETR450 trains for Italian State Railways was complete in early 1987. They are due to enter service in 1988.

further than a prototype with a dummy body, while a projected high speed electric multiple-unit designated Ale541 (later Ale481) hardly passed beyond the drawing board. Nor did the *Pendolino* seem the answer.

Construction of the *direttissima* continued in fits and starts with allocations of funds being rapidly exhausted as inflation took its toll of money values. Opening of the Orte tunnel on 29 April 1980 bridged the last gap on the southern half of the line and allowed an extra 5min to be shaved off Rome–Florence timings as trains no longer had to trundle round the tunnel on the bypass between Bivio Gallese and Orte north at 120km/h. No longer was the *direttissima* the first European shinkansen, for SNCF was getting ready to inaugurate the Paris Sud-Est TGV line in September 1981.

Work continued sporadically, and the stagnation was enlivened only briefly by further battles over the routing of the line into Florence. In 1982 it was agreed that a deviation starting in the San Donato tunnel would continue with only one short section on the surface and a tunnel into the centre of Florence with a station below the FS terminus at Santa Maria Novella. From there it would continue underground to emerge north of the city with a new section providing a link to the main line to Bologna at Prato. This massive addition to the original scheme inevitably put off completion until the 1990s.

## Prospects transformed

But in 1983–84 there were whisperings of change. The country was entering a rare period of political stability (average term of office for an Italian government since the war was less than 12 months), and the Ministry of Transport was busy with proposals to free FS from the traditional shackles of state control. A change in legal status was to transform FS from a department of the Ministry of Transport into a fully-fledged state corporation, and Transport Minister Claudio Signorile was carefully grooming FS for the switch, which eventually took effect on 1 January 1986.

For the first time in its history the FS management had a measure of commercial freedom, and the new team at once set out to carve a secure niche in the transport marketplace. Central to their endeavours were plans for high speed operations that had been nurtured behind the scenes. Among them featured a bold attempt to recover the lost prestige of the *direttissima*.

The traction engineers had not been idle. Some of the E444 loco-

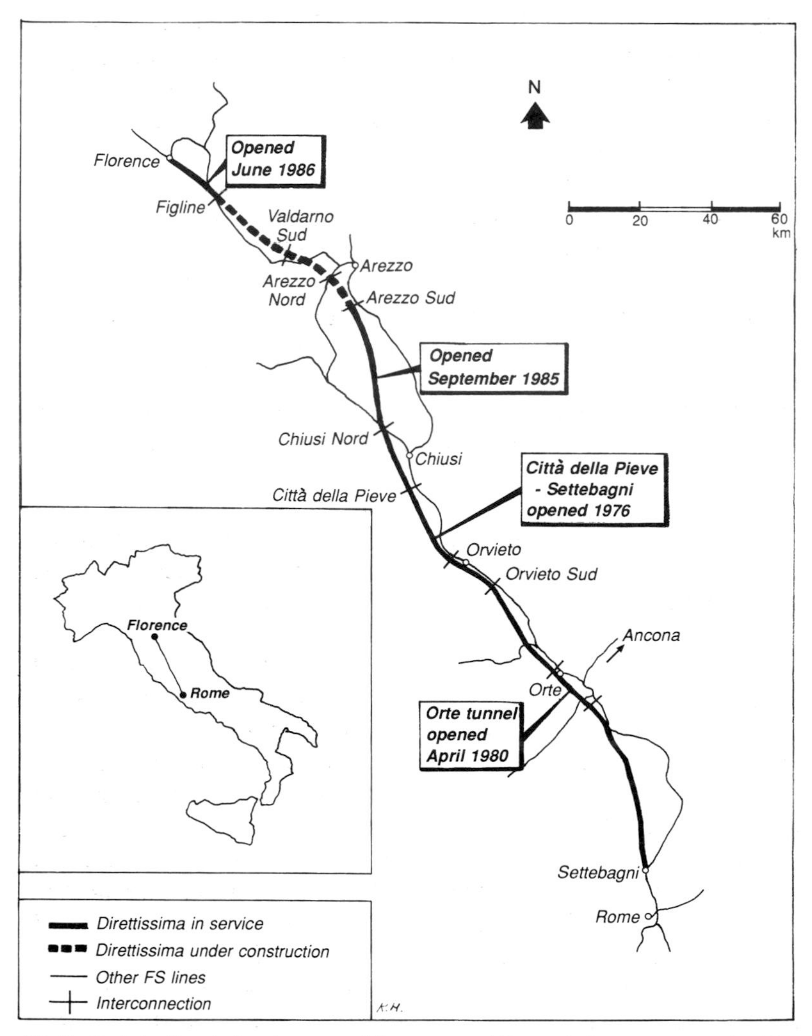


*Fig 7.* Italy's *direttissima* between Florence and Rome is interconnected with the old line at frequent intervals, giving the operators the flexibility of a four-track main line.

motives and the Ale601 multiple-units were being modified to allow them to run at 200km/h. And in 1984 the *Pendolino* was put through another series of 250km/h trials on the *direttissima*. Also on the drawing board was a new high speed Bo-Bo locomotive design, the E402, with three-phase traction motors.

Out of the blue FS called a press conference in Rome on 23 May 1985. Journalists were invited to inspect the newly spruced-up *Pen-*

*dolino* awaiting them at Termini station. Engineers in charge of the train obligingly tilted individual coaches for the benefit of photographers while the train stood at the platform. Enthusiastic executives from Fiat explained that the tilting train had been perfected and was ready for series production.

To prove just how effective the *Pendolino*'s tilt system was the set made a dash up the old main line to Chiusi, hammering through sharp curves at up to 150km/h, about 30 per cent faster than other trains. The view from the cab showed the track appearing to shoot away from under the train as the tilt swung the body up to 10° into the curves. A camera mounted in the nose conveyed this dramatic impression to a screen installed in one of the intermediate cars where even the hardier members of the fraternity were finding it easier to stay seated than attempt to wander up and down with the floor apparently moving underneath their feet.

Speed peaked at 170km/h on the outward trip with the tilt mechanism functioning faultlessly. There were visible signs of relief among the passengers who stepped out for a breather at Chiusi before the return run, and several people I spoke to confessed to feelings of nausea.

All the queasiness was swiftly forgotten as the *Pendolino* roared back to Rome on the new line (where there was no need to tilt), its cab crammed with journalists and television crews watching the speedometer as it crept up to 250km/h, briefly touching 255km/h. This was not a record as FS staff assured their guests that the *Pendolino* had earlier achieved 260km/h.

Back in Rome FS Director-General Luigi Misiti announced that a 90 billion lire contract had been placed with Fiat for four 'Son of *Pendolino*' sets, each of 11 cars. Against all expectations after 10 years of trials and tribulations the *Pendolino* had come of age.

The four ETR450 sets being delivered in 1987–88 are closely modelled on the original with the same concept of longitudinally mounted underfloor traction motors each driving the inner axle of a bogie. Chopper control is fitted and axleload is a mere 12 tonnes.

Except for the seventh car which houses the main catering facilities, all vehicles are powered. They are arranged in electrical pairs fed from 'castle' mounted pantographs on the fifth and sixth cars. Light alloy bodies have full air-conditioning with a complete train offering 450 first class seats.

Objectives set for the ETR450 are to run at 250km/h on the *direttissima* and to achieve a matching increase in speed on conventional lines thanks to fast curving. The first of the four trains was due to be rolled out for trials in summer 1987 with handover the following September. The second set is to be in FS hands by January 1988 with the last two following in April and May respectively.

Further evidence of the FS desire to make up lost time came in July 1986 with a 201.1 billion lire follow-on order for six more ETR450 sets. To be delivered between mid-1988 and the end of 1989, they will permit introduction of two daily trips between Rome and Venice in a 4hr 30min timing and stepping up of the Rome–Milan high speed service to provide three daily return workings.

The order also embraced a quartet of five-car *mini-pendolini* intended to pare journey times to the south. FS rolling stock & traction director Emilio Cardini in 1986 expected that the Rome–Bari trip would be 4hr 30min and Rome–Reggio de Calabria around 6hr. Fastest timing for the Bari run in 1986 was 5hr 34min and for Reggio 7hr 25min. Each set will have a continuous rating of 2,670kW and a speed ceiling of 200km/h.

But FS was conscious too of the need for an immediate speed-up to the north where airlines were eroding the market position of the first-class only TEE trains linking Rome with the northern industrial capital of Milan. By June 1985 FS had modified the first of 13 Tortoise locomotives for 200km/h running by fitting them with cab signalling and a different gear ratio, reclassifying them as E447. As an experiment, they were to haul a pair of Rome–Florence *rapidi* in commercial service at 200km/h on the *direttissima*. It was nearly 10 years since the 250km/h line had opened.

On 13 November 1985 the *Pendolino* made a test run between Rome and Milan, calling intermediately only at Firenze Campo di Marte in an attempt to simulate the future timing planned for the new trains. On board were FS and Fiat executives, the general manager of Swiss Federal Railways and a number of design engineers working on the ICE train which a few days later was to set a new German speed record.

Departure was late (a not unusual occurrence in Italy), and the special left at 10.19 instead of 09.45. A 5hr timing had been scheduled to give a Milan arrival at 14.45. Actual arrival was only 5 min down at 14.50, giving an overall timing of 4hr 31min for the 609km trip. The average speed between Rome and Florence was 153km/h with a maximum of around 220km/h; 200km/h was attained between Bologna and Milan.

As much as 42min had been lost because of engineering works and adverse signals so that a net timing of 3hr 49min was theoretically possible. This performance seemed to indicate that the 4hr timing envisaged for the two return workings by the ETR450 sets between Rome and Milan in 1988 was just feasible, but FS subsequently revised this to 4hr 30min.

## The Italian TAV

Misiti's revelations about the *super-Pendolino* on 23 May 1985 were but the first part of the story. The *super-Pendolino* was just an interim step on the way to the *Treno ad Alta Velocita* (TAV), a full-blooded high speed train capable of attaining 270km/h on the *direttissima*. Officially classed by FS as ETR500, it was to have a top speed of 300km/h.

The timescale for the ETR500 stretches into the 1990s as there would be little point in building such a sophisticated train without somewhere to run it. When the plans were announced in May 1985 FS still had only the southern half of the *direttissima* open to traffic. But progress was at last tangible.

The next section of the line, the 52km from Città della Pieve to Arezzo Sud, was years behind schedule when it finally opened on 29 September 1985. This time there was no party and trains began running over the new section almost unnoticed. FS decided that although the extra tranche of new line would allow a few minutes to be pared off timings it would be preferable to wait until 1986 when the 17km approach to Florence from Valdarno Nord would open too. The two new sections combined permitted a full 30min to be cut out of the timetable.

On 30 May 1986 FS marked the occasion by staging a demonstration run from Rome to Florence with an E447 and five *Gran Conforto* TEE coaches. The trip also commemorated the official start of 200km/h running on the *direttissima* with several Class 447 hauled TEEs and *rapidi* running at the new ceiling. Thus FS became the sixth railway in the world to join the 200 club after JNR, SNCF, DB, BR and SZD (Soviet Railways).

At Florence FS held a press conference outlining its strategy for high speeds. In 1988 a regular interval timetable would be introduced between Rome and Florence with trains worked by a mix of ETR450 *super-Pendolini* and Class 447 hauled *rapidi*, some with new Type Z1 second class coaches. These would be superseded in 1990 by the ETR500 sets and Class E402 locomotives. A massive 12,500 billion lire was to be spent on about 100 TAVs and more new line construction, so that by the turn of the century a 4hr 35min timing would be possible between Milan and Naples with Milan–Rome slashed to 3hr.

In the meantime huge efforts are being made to close the *direttissima* chapter. After the Florence approach route was inaugurated in 1986 a 45km gap remained in the middle between Arezzo Sud and Valdarno Nord. Right at the beginning controversy had raged over the routing of the line near Arezzo. It was not until July 1985 that contracts for the 19km from Arezzo Sud to Laterina were let, leaving the final 26km dependent on a 'refinancing' arrangement that was to release a further 350 billion lire.

## TAV prototypes

With the *direttissima* once more enjoying top priority, rolling stock director Cardini got his act together quickly. On the basis of preliminary design work carried out by his staff and Italian rolling stock builders in 1984 he had to come up with a mature design of train able to run at speeds never seriously considered in Italy before.

He drew up a programme for the ETR500 aimed at reducing the development time. While his engineering team was proceeding with detailed design, they would be able to draw on valuable experience with real life high speed operation thanks to the *super-Pendolino* sets.

The fundamentals had been defined by September 1984 in what Cardini termed the train architecture. The TAV was to have two power cars enclosing 12 trailers. The Type E404 power cars would have the same three-phase electrical equipment as five Class E402 Bo-Bo locomotives ordered in 1985, when a dummy had been built to test some of the equipment. Continuous power rating was 5,100kW (4,000kW on the E404) and maximum speed 220km/h.

Next step was to develop a prototype ETR500. Cardini's method was to have not one but two prototypes, each with different objectives. The first, consisting of a single power car and instrumented trailer coded ETRX500, was due to start running trials in 1987. Its main purpose is to evaluate the trailer and power bogies which incorporate a novel type of transmission with a flexible drive surrounding the axle; this transmission includes elements made from titanium, an import from the aerospace industry. This train will also serve to test current collection and braking.

Practically all other tests are to be carried out on ETRY500, the second prototype. This will consist of two power cars and three intermediate trailers fitted with passenger accommodation and will run in revenue service to assess passenger reactions. All the data collected from the two prototypes will be used to define the design of production version, due to carry fare-paying passengers in the early 1990s.

Wheeled in to head the design team was Sergio Pinin Farina, son of the famous sports car stylist Battista Farina. It was the first time that FS had turned to outside help for rolling stock design.

There remained the question of where the ETR500 was to run at its design speed. Attaining the 3hr Rome–Milan timing implied massive improvements north of Florence. In 1985 Transport Minister Claudio Signorile, the architect of the transfer of FS away from the government, began talking about a transport master plan. Drawn up in 1983, it spent the next three years being scrutinised by a government commission.

One of the cornerstones of this ambitious plan is what Italian newsmen call the 'Great T'. This is a project for creating two super railways along the principal transport axes of a country which is shaped rather like a Wellington boot with the top folded down. The vertical trunk of the T would be a *direttissima* stretching from Naples north to Milan, with the cross bar being a line of similar standard binding together the great industrial conurbations of the north – Turin, Milan and Venice. The master plan also contained a proposal to build a new line north to the Brenner pass where a new base tunnel would be built into Austria. At 1985 prices all this was costed at 34,000 billion lire.

After the earlier fiascos with the *direttissima*, to embark on such an ambitious plan would seem to be inviting massive criticism. But the relative political stability of Italy in the mid-1980s is pushing the reinvigorated FS towards ambitious goals. FS is a serious contender to become the third railway in the world to operate at 270km/h.

# 13

# EUROPE CATCHES THE TGV

When the final third of the Paris–Sud-Est line was inaugurated in September 1983 the TGV concept had already taken root among the French population. Far from protesting against new high speed railways, towns and regions were clamouring to have their own TGV lines. A Mr Adrian Zeller, for instance, had set up something called the *Association pour la Réalisation du TGV-Est Européen*, appointing himself as President. It did not take him long to win the support of other politicians in eastern France.

Zeller's zeal obviously washed off somewhere, for in April 1984 President Mitterrand let slip a remark about 'a TGV line from our capital, passing through Lorraine, to West Germany and Frankfurt.' Zeller leapt into action, citing a feasibility study which was picked up by *Le Monde* on May 3. For the sum of Fr10bn, eastern France would enjoy a service of 114 TGVs a day worked by 34 trainsets. Unfortunately these figures had no sound basis, and SNCF dismissed them as 'not correlating with any official study'.

Persistence was not one of the things that Zeller was short of, and on 25 July 1984 the French government set up a commission with a brief to study a TGV line to the Lorraine, publicly acknowledging the international dimension of the scheme at the Franco-German summit meeting seven months later.

Preliminary details of what rapidly became known as TGV-Est were completed within a few months. Journey time for the Paris–Strasbourg run would be whittled down from 3hr 50min to 2hr 10min, with traffic in 1995 estimated at 8 to 12 million passengers, depending on the choice of route. A working party put forward two routes, both following the Paris–Strasbourg main line for the first 30km. One passed north of Reims and between Metz and Nancy, the other ran south of Vitry-le-François and Nancy.

A further study in 1986 suggested a branch off the Paris–Sud-Est line near Aisy to Vesoul. The present route from Vesoul to Belfort would be beefed up to allow some high speed running, so giving Belfort, Montbéliard, Mulhouse and Basle a high speed link to Paris.

The TGV-Est route passing between Metz and Nancy needed 384km of new construction, billed in 1985 at Fr10.4 billion. But the rate of return of about 3 or 4 per cent for SNCF is not likely to persuade the French government to rush ahead.

The best chance for TGV-Est would seem to be in the context of an international high speed network with a Mannheim–Saarbrücken new line in Germany meeting TGV-Est at the frontier. Were this built, the Paris–Stuttgart timing would be pruned from 6hr 10min in 1986 to 3hr 50min.

## Extension to the south

Early in 1987 greater interest was being shown by the transport ministry in a scheme to extend the Paris–Sud-Est line round Lyon. SNCF was able to demonstrate a 10 per cent rate of return on the investment cost of Fr4.1 billion which would buy 122km of new line from Civrieux, 22km north of Lyon Part-Dieu to St Marcel-les-Valence, 10km northeast of Valence on the line to Grenoble. Design parameters would be similar to those for Paris–Sud-Est, except that 300km/h running would be a sine qua non.

One incentive was the choice of the French alps as the venue for the 1992 winter Olympics, but also important to SNCF was growing congestion on the lines through and south of Lyon. Despite the availability of a double track main line on each side of the Rhône valley, SNCF says that the left bank route is one of the busiest double track lines on its network.

Having been presented with the proposals late in 1986, Transport Minister Jacques Douffiagues saw fit to remark that the chances of the extension being built would be enhanced if local or regional authorities chipped in. For the line to be ready by 1992, a decision would have to be taken in 1987. Although the whole line might eventually be built, and bring SNCF's long-term objective of a 4hr Paris–Marseilles timing a little nearer, it is probable that only the first part as far as St Quentin-Fallavier on the Lyons–Grenoble main line will go ahead before 1990; price tag for chopping 20 min off the fastest Paris–Grenoble timing would be Fr1.4bn.

In fact, SNCF readily admits that it wants a TGV line all the way to

Marseilles, but it is aware that agricultural interests further south would pose extremely tricky problems. The junction with the Grenoble–Valence line will actually be designed to allow for eventual extension of the TGV route further south.

Surely the least likely of all France's TGV plans is that suggested by the Dordogne senator Lucien Delmas in February 1986. Asked by the Prime Minister to draw up a report on what changes were needed in southern France to handle increased trade with Spain and Portugal following their acceptance in the EEC the previous month, Delmas suggested a TGV link between Montpellier and Bordeaux via Toulouse.

## Spain joins the club

Although Delmas' scheme is certainly far-fetched, the question of better links to Spain is important. It will become more so as Spain grows within the Common Market, which has already brought significant change to the Iberian peninsula.

Spain's 1.668m (5ft 6in) broad gauge State Railway (RENFE) had for some time been struggling to adapt to changing market conditions, with improvements centred on a 1,200 billion pesetas 10 year investment plan agreed in 1981. This ambitious programme was discredited in 1984 as being investment for the sake of technical improvement rather than as a commercial proposition.

Unhappy with this state of affairs, the socialist government that took office in 1982 appointed a more commercially conscious management team in a bid to rein in RENFE's runaway finances. There was considerable upheaval in the Madrid headquarters, but within a year substantial progress was made on the financial front, and RENFE also advanced technically.

In July 1985 RENFE announced a programme of high speed trials that entailed upgrading three sections of line for 200km/h running. It had two classes of diesel Talgo locomotive able to attain this speed, while purchase of several series of high-quality inter-city coaches closely modelled on the latest designs in the rest of Western Europe ensured that there was no shortage of suitable rolling stock. By the summer of 1986 RENFE had enough experience to raise the speed ceiling on substantial sections of the Madrid–Barcelona main line to 160km/h, and similar accelerations followed in May 1987 on the Madrid–Hendaye route.

Credit was given where it was due, and in return for efforts to raise productivity and tighten up on efficiency generally the government rewarded RENFE with an investment programme worth more than the one which had been scrapped.

Minister of Transport Abel Caballero announced in November 1986 that his government had completed plans for what he described as 'the biggest railway investment of the century', with a whopping 2,100 billion pesetas to be spent by 2000. The plans were geared specifically to inter-city passenger services that would give RENFE a competitive edge over airlines and private cars. No less than three new lines were included in a bid to bring down inter-city journey times to cities on the northern littoral and in the southwest.

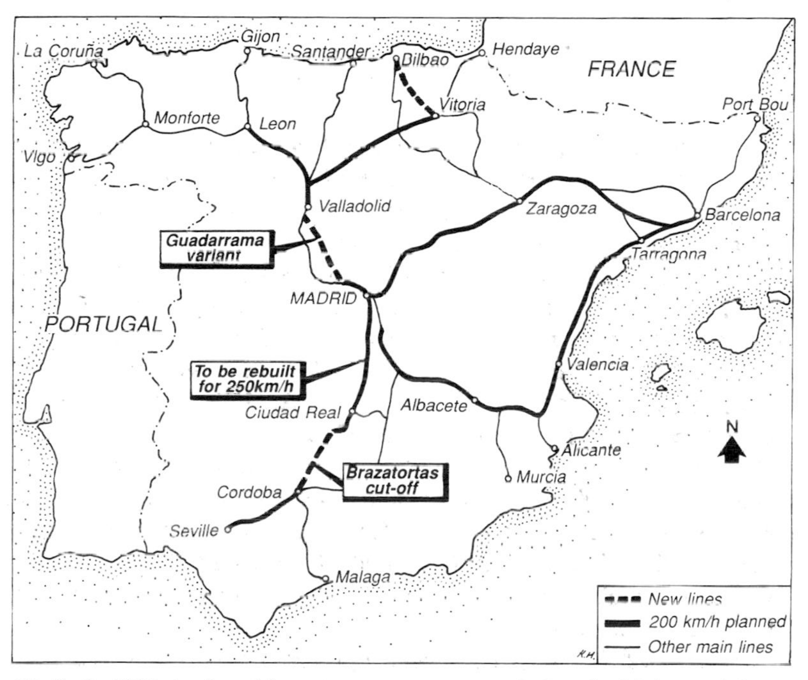


*Fig 8.* In 1986 the Spanish government announced plans for high speed lines and services on principal inter-city routes.

Two of the three new lines will be designed for 250km/h. Planning is most advanced with the so-called Brazatortas cut-off, a 105km cut through the Sierra Morena that will shorten the route from the capital to Cordoba and Seville. This 45 billion pesetas line will save southbound expresses the long drag over the steeply graded Despeñaperros pass on the main line through Manzanares which is partly single track. By early 1987 the Ministry of Transport was negotiating for land purchases, and confidently predicting a start on construction for early 1988, even though the government had yet to promulgate the legislation for the overall plan.

Construction of the cut-off will be accompanied by complete rebuilding of the Madrid–Badajoz main line between Parla and Ciudad Real to permit 250km/h running. From Ciudad Real to the town of Puertallano 200km/h will be possible. Just east of here lies Brazatortas, start of the new line which strikes southwest to join the Madrid–Cordoba main line at Alcolea, 8km east of Cordoba. The double-track route will be electrified at 25kV 50Hz, demanding dual-system rolling stock capable also of operation on Spain's 3kV dc system that has yet to be developed. Target date for opening is 1992–93, when high speed services will put Cordoba no more than 2hr away from the capital.

The second new line, termed the Guadarrama variant, consists of a deep cut in tunnel under the Sierra Guadarrama north and west of Madrid. This will leave the Madrid–Avila main line at Las Zorreras and join the Medina–Palencia line at Valdestillas, about 18km south of the famous cathedral and university city of Valladolid. The Ministry rates the return on this line at 14 per cent. Together with a cut-off through the Basque hills from Vitoria to Bilbao, journey time from the capital to the industrial north will be reduced by 2hr.

The new lines will be accompanied by massive upgrading of other trunk routes, particularly in the Madrid–Barcelona–Valencia triangle. The long drag down the coast from Barcelona to Valencia will become a 200km/h inter-city artery, with matching improvement on the lines from Madrid to Zaragoza, Barcelona and Albacete.

In 1987 RENFE possessed no stock capable of 250km/h, but further development of the Talgo concept might produce one of Europe's most interesting high speed trains. The problem in this case would be motive power, as an axleload lower than the 20 tonnes of the latest Talgo diesels would be essential. Perhaps the *Basculante* will be resurrected, but a broad gauge Spanish TGV may yet surprise us.

## Swiss high speed plans

By the mid 1980s the TGV effect was spreading all along France's frontiers. Even in Switzerland where the opportunities for high speed running are heavily restrained by inhospitable terrain there was profound interest. After all, the Swiss benefited from direct TGV services right at the start in 1981. Explosive growth of rail traffic on the Geneva–Paris axis followed the TGV launch in that year, and when the timings for the 551km trip were pared to 3hr 30min both Swissair and Air France were forced to review their services and fares. Meanwhile rail traffic went from strength to strength. In five years it burgeoned by 400 per cent, and an extra daily round trip was welded into the timetable.

Tri-current TGVs supplanted locomotive hauled trains on the 508km Paris–Lausanne route in January 1984, and two years later traffic was up by 70 per cent – although this had to be weighed against a drop in through traffic from Paris to Milan because passengers did not like the change at Lausanne, even though it was a simple matter of crossing the platform.

The Swiss were particularly interested by the TGV because they too had plans for high speed lines, although speeds much above 200km/h were not envisaged. The ceiling in Switzerland was 140km/h for many years, and only in January 1986 was 160km/h permitted over a 20km stretch of the Simplon main line through the Valais where new signalling had been installed. Apart from that, Swiss Federal Railways (SBB) possessed only four locomotives (the Re4/4 IV prototypes) capable of 160km/h.

Proposals for the Swiss high speed lines surfaced in a document published in 1977 called the Swiss Integral Concept of Transport. In December that year the authors recommended that two new high speed lines should be built as the main plank of a strategy aimed at reversing the decline in rail's market share. One route was to run east–west on the busy Lausanne–Berne–Zurich–St Gallen artery, the other between Basle and Olten on the north–south axis that feeds into the Gotthard main line. The report noted that a high speed line through the Alps in the form of a Gotthard base tunnel would not be justified until after 2000.

Inevitably, the government appointed another set of experts to evaluate the proposals, and it was not until 1983 that the next report appeared. In the meantime public opinion had come out against the new lines in their original form, although not against them in principle. But new proposals were to hand in the shape of something altogether more radical that was to win the support of large sectors of the Swiss public – and the politicians.

Four new lines formed the keystone of a rail strategy dreamed up by a nexus of far-thinking individuals among the higher echelons of Swiss Federal Railways' management. The brainchild of Samuel Stähli and Hans Meiner, Rail 2000 was a concept based on the premise of running trains not as fast as possible but as fast as necessary to

*continued on page 164*

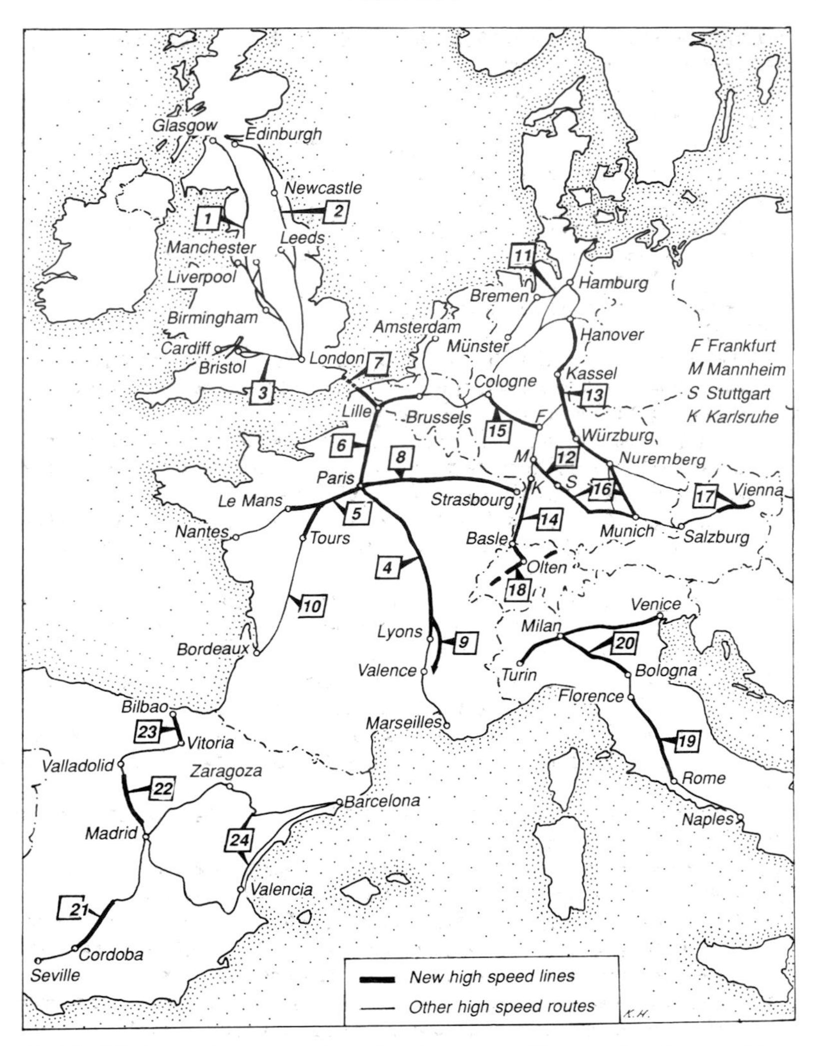


*Fig* 9. High speed routes and services in western Europe showing new lines in service, under construction or planned.

Key to figures:
1 Selected trains in the group of services on BR's electrified West Coast main line run at 177km/h.
2 On BR's East Coast main line 200km/h diesel High Speed Trains will be replaced by electric services from 1988. Edinburgh will be reached by 1991. The speed limit will be raised in the long term to 225km/h.
3 On BR's main line to Bristol and South Wales 200km/h HSTs began running in 1976.
4 The Paris–Sud-Est line opened with TGVs running at 260km/h in 1981,

but the limit was raised to 270km/h in 1983. A further increase to 290 or 300km/h is possible by 1990.
5 TGV-Atlantique, the world's first 300km/h railway, will open in two stages in 1989 and 1990.
6 TGV-Nord, France's third high speed line from Paris to Brussels and the Channel Tunnel, is due to open simultaneously with the Tunnel in 1993. Extensions to Cologne and Amsterdam are planned in the long term.
7 The Channel Tunnel has a design speed of 200km/h. By mid-1988 BR will submit to the government options for raising speed and capacity between the Tunnel and London.
8 TGV-Est from Paris to Strasbourg will not be built until completion of TGV-Nord.
9 Engineering design of 122km extension of Paris–Sud-Est line past Lyons to St-Marcel-les-Valence was completed early in 1987; SNCF has long term plans to extend it eventually to Marseilles.
10 Paris–Bordeaux main line used by locomotive-hauled electric trains at 200km/h. TGV-Atlantique trains to Bordeaux will be allowed to run at 220km/h on the old line between Tours and Bordeaux.
11 Many sections of line in West Germany are being upgraded for 200km/h running. About 2,000km of route will be cleared for 200km/h by the end of the century.
12 Mannheim–Stuttgart *Neubaustrecke* under construction; first section between Mannheim and Hockenheim opened May 1987, but 250km/h running not envisaged until 1990–91.
13 Hanover–Würzburg Neubaustrecke under construction will open in stages commencing 1988; 250km/h running to start in 1990–91.
14 Karlsruhe–Offenburg–Basle high speed line (193km) will blend new construction with upgrading of old line. Construction authorised to start in 1987.
15 (Cologne)–Bonn–Frankfurt *Neubaustrecke* planned for construction in 1990s; route defined early 1987.
16 New high speed routes planned between Stuttgart, Ulm and Munich and from Würzburg to Nuremberg and Munich; routes to be defined.
17 Proposal for 200km/h high speed route from Vienna to Salzburg includes new line to St Pölten with more new sections further west; a similar plan exists for upgrading the main line south from Vienna to Graz.
18 Construction of four sections of new line in Switzerland for 200km/h depend on outcome of referendum likely to be held at end of 1987.
19 Rome–Florence *direttissima* partly in service; completion planned by 1990.
20 Construction of high speed lines in northern Italy included in long term government transport infrastructure programme.
21 Brazatortas cut-off to be built for 250km/h has high priority in railway investment programme drawn up by Spanish government in 1986–87.
22 Guadarramay high speed line included in government investment plan will permit major cuts in journey time from Madrid to northern Spain.
23 Vitoria–Bilbao cut-off will connect industrial area to rest of Spanish high speed network.
24 Madrid–Barcelona, Madrid–Valencia and Barcelona–Valencia routes to be rebuilt to allow 200km/h running.

achieve given objectives, in particular to provide a fully-interconnecting network of services right across Switzerland on an hourly interval basis.

In an ideal situation every city interchange station would be a little less than 1hr distant from the next one, allowing an hourly cycle of services that connect at the same time every hour in all directions. As several Swiss cities were already approximately 1hr apart, Stähli and his colleagues set out to make the others equidistant in time too. This was where the new lines came in.

The strategists calculated that four new lines would suffice, allowing high speed running over short sections that would bring journey times down to the even hour, for example between Berne and Zurich. The four lines were Vauderens–Villars sur Glâne, Mattstetten (Berne)–Olten, Muttenz (Basle)–Olten and Zurich Airport–Winterthur.

Rail 2000 proponents envisaged a speed of 200km/h on the new lines, but in 1986 SBB asked the Swiss companies who built their locomotives to come up with a design able to haul inter-city trains at up to 230km/h, General Manager Hans Eisenring commented that if his Loco 2000 could run at 230 rather than 200km/h it might be possible to build shorter new lines as a trade-off, still achieving the Rail 2000 objectives. This locomotive will have three-phase traction motors and control circuitry featuring gate turn-off thyristors, and SBB plans to have a first batch in service by about 1990.

By then a start should have been made on the new high speed lines, SBB having marshalled considerable high level support for its concept in 1985 and 1986. A unanimous vote at State Council level in summer 1986 in favour of the route of the most controversial of the lines, that between Mattstetten and Olten, underlined this political support. But before the lines can go ahead the bill must clear both houses of the Swiss parliament and was to be submitted to a referendum in December 1987.

## Austrian initiatives

Interest in high speed running even spread to the tranquil hills of Austria, where plans for two high speed lines began to gel in the 1970s. One stretched 108km from Vienna's Westbahnhof to Amstetten, with 90km of new construction, much of it in tunnel. With 250km/h running and massive upgrading and realignment further west, it would allow a Tyrolean returning from festivities in Vienna to be in his home town of Innsbruck in just 3hr. The Vienna–Salzburg run would be similarly slashed from 3hr 10min to 2hr 5min.

The second route ran south from Vienna with a 33km new line embracing a new tunnel under the Semmering pass. This would shorten the run to Graz, and with high speed running would cut 60min off the journey to the Styrian capital to give a 1hr 35min schedule. These proposals were taken seriously enough for Austrian Federal Railways (ÖBB) to commission a study from American consultants Arthur D Little into high performance railways in 1985–86.

The report was finished by autumn 1986, although its contents were not made public. It was nonetheless clear that it favoured the idea of a souped up line from Vienna to the west, although it suggested that 200km/h might be fast enough for ÖBB's inter-city traffic to get a substantial boost. Given that Austria has a political need to provide something for the civil engineering industry following abandonment of a programme to build nuclear power stations, it seems just possible that high speed trains may one day traverse Mozart's town en route for the Vienna woods.

## More *Neubaustrecken*

On 10 January 1987 the West German Transport Ministry in Bonn gave DB the all-clear to order an initial batch of 10 IC-Express sets, later revising this to 41 sets worth DM1.5 billion enabling DB to issue letters of intent in September 1987. By this time DB was making very substantial progress with its Mannheim–Stuttgart and Hanover–Würzburg *Neubaustrecken*, and plans for more high speed routes were no longer taboo. In fact, on 21 January 1987, Transport Minister Werner Dollinger announced the go-ahead for a third *Neubaustrecke* covering the 193km up the Rhine valley from Karlsruhe through Offenburg to Basle.

Pleased with the DB management's progress in halting runaway finances during the 1980s, the Ministry had earlier acceded to practically all the requests for new lines that the DB management could possibly conceive. They were formulated in the 1985 review of the National Transport Infrastructure Plan. Out of a total budget for the 10 years to 1995 of DM126 billion, DM35 billion was allocated to railway improvements. DB had no less than 33 projects in mind, some of them for entirely new lines, others such as Munich–Nuremberg and Munich–Stuttgart being a mix of new construction and heavy upgrading.

Most significant of all the 1985 proposals was revival of the Cologne–Frankfurt project, which DB now envisaged would be a passenger-only line. The traffic potential for a high speed rail link between the industry of the Ruhr and the business centre in Frankfurt is high, with a line along the route of the present motorway through Limburg giving a journey time of 1hr. Priced at DM5.4 billion, it would have to traverse the difficult terrain of the Westerwald, demanding major bridge and tunnel work. It is barely conceivable that the line would not serve the West German capital at Bonn, but there was much squabbling about it missing out Coblence further up the Rhine. Coblence has now accepted that it will not be on the high speed network, but the lengthy two-stage planning process means that a start on construction is unlikely before 1990.

Already DB has 470km of line where 200km/h is permitted. If all the plans in the 1985 transport infrastructure plan are brought to fruition, DB will have 2,000km passed for 200km/h by the end of the century. About 425km will be worked at 250km/h, with the possibility of this ceiling being raised to 270km/h by the mid-1990s.

# 14
# THE FRONTIERS OF HIGH SPEED

Anyone in the business of exporting high speed trains has a pretty thankless task. Perhaps most successful is the British HST whose Antipodean cousins the XPTs (Chapter 5) have revitalised inter city travel in New South Wales. But their 160km/h maximum hardly qualifies them for a high speed rosette.

Not that high speed development in New South Wales will stop with XPT. In 1986 the State Rail Authority invited tenders for a new generation of 14 High Performance Trains (HPT). Their specification calls for options to draw power at 1.5kV dc from overhead wires in the Sydney suburban area, and if plans to electrify other lines in New South Wales go ahead, they may have traction equipment for 25kV 50Hz too. Intended to take over premier services such as the *Intercapital Daylight Express* to Melbourne, the HPTs may well be able to exceed 160km/h.

The opportunity for HPTs to run at 160km/h plus does not yet exist, but there are ambitious plans for a high speed line from Sydney to Melbourne. The idea was floated in 1984 by the Chairman of the Commonwealth Scientific & Industrial Research Organisation, Dr Paul Wild. At the time little attention was given to his proposal, but two years later he grabbed the headlines with his concept for a Very Fast Train (VFT). He had by this time transferred his allegiance to a trio of private interests which embraced the New South Wales arm of a Japanese construction company, the Australian transport group Elders IXL and the TNT company. The three were willing to stake $A600,000 on a 'pre-feasibility study' for the VFT which they estimated could cut Sydney–Melbourne travel time to a breathtaking 3hr, including a stop at Canberra. That represents an average speed of 289km/h, demanding a maximum of 350km/h.

Wild estimated construction cost to be $A2.9 billion on the assumption that a start could be made in 1989 once detailed design had been completed. Drawing on French and Japanese technology, VFT

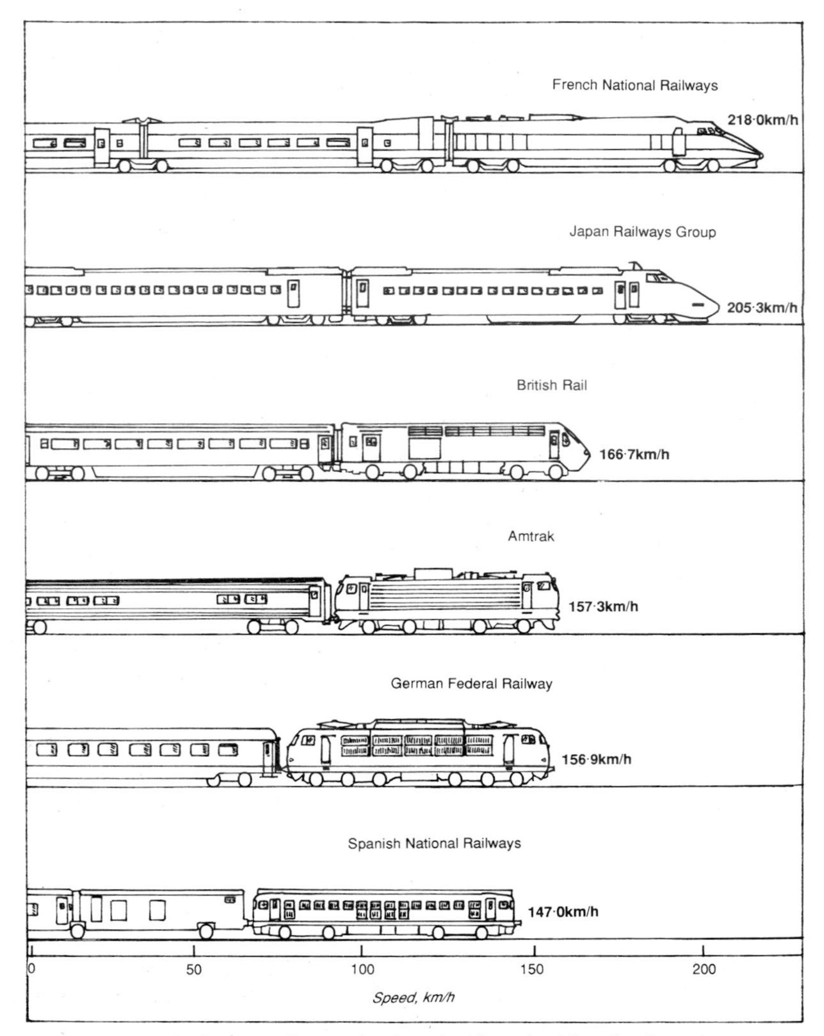


*Fig 10.* The six fastest railways in the world ranked by the fastest start-to-stop average speed for an advertised service in the summer 1987 timetable. Those exceeding 200km/h are confined to France and Japan, but British Rail's diesel powered HSTs take a well-deserved bronze medal. The Talgo train in sixth place is remarkable, as Spanish National Railways only began 160km/h scheduled services in 1986. Data for this diagram was compiled by Dr Colin Taylor of Queensland University.

would entail 796km of new double track electrified at 25kV 50Hz. At each end of the route trains would share existing railway rights-of-way, just as the TGV does in Paris and Lyon. With an alignment through Canberra, at present served by two trains a day on a 106km branch from Goulburn, route length would be 868km. This is 92km shorter than the present line through Wagga Wagga and Albury, over which the fastest schedule in 1986 was around 12hr for 961km.

An intermediate link to the SRANSW network at Goulburn would permit XPTs or HPTs bound for Wagga Wagga and Albury to exploit the new line, so bringing high speed travel to cities well off the VFT route.

The VFT line would have 3.5 per cent grades and a minimum curve radius of 7,000 metres, the same as West Germany's *Neubaustrecken*. An initial fleet of 10 passenger VFTs would be built, together with five freight units similar to the French postal TGVs. By using special high speed rolling stock for freight the VFT route would not suffer from pathing problems which required the Germans to build passing loops every 20km on the *Neubaustrecken*.

Wild hopes the first VFTs will roll in 1995, taking a substantial share of the 10 million Sydney–Melbourne annual journeys. But this is peanuts compared with the Tokaido–Sanyo shinkansen (128 million passengers a year) and even the TGV (16 million a year). Two separate consultants have the job of looking at the market, and their conclusions will doubtless determine whether Wild's dream will be realised. His idea of high speed freight could help to bolster earnings, but whether investors would recoup the capital in 12 years from opening is a crucial question. If Wild can produce evidence that they will, he believes the line would be built and run entirely by private interests.

## North American corridors

No country offers greater opportunities for high speed trains than the USA. There are several corridors where the population density and the distance between large cities fit within the high speed rail bracket. But these corridors are at present served by frequent flights which the Americans treat as bus services. As yet no high speed trains exist outside the Northeast Corridor. Even here, experience has not been propitious.

The *Metroliner* debut in particular (Chapter 3) was pretty disastrous. E. T. Harley, the Pennsylvania Railroad's last assistant chief mechanical officer, locomotives, writing in the introduction to *The Pennsylvania Railroad* by Don Ball Jr (Elm Tree Books, Chester, Vermont, 1986) blames 'a development timetable built around President Johnson's re-election and unrealistic specifications from the Office of High Speed Ground Transportation in Washington', but he does admit that the *Metroliners* were eventually successful. Yet Amtrak paid dearly to keep them up to scratch – sometimes a quarter of the fleet was out of service.

Rebuilding them was not the answer – it was simply too expensive, as Amtrak discovered after sending two snack bar and two coach class cars back to General Electric in 1973 under a research contract paid for by the Federal Railroad Administration. They came back with a massive roof pod of electrical equipment transferred from under the floor; while most bugs had been eliminated, the price was as high as buying the original cars.

Amtrak set out on a hunt. First it bought six RTG gas turbine sets from France in 1973. These showed sufficient promise to prompt an order for seven more, this time an Americanised version of the same design built locally by Rohr Industries under licence from France's ANF.

The choice of turbotrains was exceedingly unfortunate timing, for the oil crisis quickly quashed hopes of any long term future for such thirsty beasts. It posed no dilemma, however, for four RTGs sold by ANF to Iran in 1975. Before they eventually succumbed to the desert and the dervishes they had a timetable booking of just 26min over a distance of 70km – a start-to-stop average of 161.5km/h.

By 1975 Amtrak has ordered the first of a fleet of locomotive-hauled cars (Amfleet) based on the *Metroliners* which were to be paired in the Northeast Corridor with 26 gigantic E60CP locomotives from the Erie shops of General Electric. The first of these monsters distinguished itself while on test by overturning a rail at 160km/h during a bout of vicious hunting. In November 1975 the FRA ruled that the E60CPs were not to exceed 129km/h – which signalled the end of that design as a high speed workhorse.

Within weeks Amtrak hired from Asea of Sweden an Rc4 thyristor-controlled four-axle locomotive converted for the North-east Corridor's 11kV 25Hz power supply. Another leasing deal followed in June 1976, this time with Alsthom–MTE of France, and in January 1977 the X996, a conversion of one of SNCF's Class 21000 six-axle monomotor-bogie locomotives, arrived on US shores. This proved almost as unsuitable for US track as the E60CPs, leaving the Rc4 victorious. The Swedish machine's capabilities swiftly earned it the nickname of Mighty Mouse – in half the weight of an E60CP, it packed the same power.

Autumn 1977 saw Amtrak approve purchase of eight AEM7 locomotives based on the Rc4, and an order was signed in January 1978, providing for them to be assembled by General Motors which held an

Asea licence. The price tag for each Mouse was a mighty $2.75 million.

With a 200km/h capability, they were destined to replace the famous and venerable GG1s as well as the E60CPs, which with the *Metroliners* were still the mainstay of the Corridor's business trains. By 1982 Amtrak had a fleet of 42 AEM7s, allowing the *Metroliners* to be relegated to suburban duties. Some were later gutted of their power equipment to work out their days as push-pull trains in California, an ignominious end indeed for what started out as a US shinkansen train.

But the Northeast Corridor needed more than just high speed rolling stock. It required complete reconstruction, and when Congress allocated $1.7 billion for just that in 1976 it did seem as though the original goals of high speed running were attainable. The job included electrification from New Haven to Boston, together with massive work on track and structures.

Not least of the dilemmas was how to maintain punctuality during the upheaval, a problem exacerbated by the mix of heavy freight, commuter and express passenger trains all competing for the same line space.

By 1978 Secretary of Transportation Brock Adams was levelling accusations of poor planning, leading to a 'redirection study' of the whole project. The result was quite simply a mess, with too many organisations being paid too much for the wrong advice, and the original objective almost forgotten. The New Haven–Boston electrification, along with replacement of the electrification and signalling dating from the 1930s between Washington and New York, was scrapped, and the rest of the programme stretched out over a much longer timescale.

About three quarters of the job had been completed by 1982, and the Mighty Mice hummed along at up to 193km/h with strings of Amfleet cars. Confusingly, they were referred to as *Metroliners*. By early 1986 the best New York–Washington timing was 2hr 49min with intermediate stops at Newark, Philadelphia, Wilmington and Baltimore. And then, two decades after the high speed plans were first laid, the moment of triumph arrived.

In October 1986 the Federal Railroad Administration cleared 157km of the Northeast Corridor for 200km/h. There was a stretch between Edison and Trenton and more on the Wilmington–Washington section. The timings were not trimmed, but as Amtrak said 'the higher speeds will help the *Metroliners* adhere to their schedules'. The USA was the seventh member of the 200 club.

## US corridors

On Amtrak's busiest line outside the Northeast Corridor between Los Angeles and San Diego there are seven trains a day each way. It was here that a high speed line came closest to being built. The 210km route was promoted by the American High Speed Rail Corporation under the chairmanship of former Amtrak President Alan Boyd who had been profoundly influenced by the shinkansen after a visit in 1979. The intention was to use a $3.1 billion shinkansen technology package with 86 eight-car trains a day carving the best Amtrak timing of 2hr 40min down to 59min.

According to a 1983 report by Arthur D Little the line would carry 36.5 million passengers a year by 1988, with annual revenue of $500m. But not long after the study was published someone pointed out that the traffic forecasts were wildly optimistic, leading to the instant demise of the High Speed Rail Corporation.

Since then other corridors have inched nearer the day when a sod might be turned over for a high speed line. Japanese technology is favoured for a 500km artery uniting Miami, Tampa and Orlando in Florida. The home state of Disneyworld sees high speed rail as a development tool that would entice property merchants away from the crowded coasts and open up inland areas.

High speed trains cutting the 390km trip between the Texan gateway cities of Dallas and Houston to 2hr or less are integral to a scheme for a golden triangle of super railways taking in San Antonio and Austin. Leading the lobbying here is a German backed consortium hoping for an export outlet for the Intercity-Express.

Right across Pennsylvania from Philadelphia to Pittsburgh (560km) runs the route of a proposed new line inspired by the Pennsylvania High Speed Intercity Rail Passenger Commission. In next-door Ohio a 400km alignment joining Cincinnati, Columbus and Cleveland has a price label of over $2 million. High speed diesels akin to the British HST are envisaged for the 450km between Chicago and the motor city of Detroit. A 400km/h maglev line between Los Angeles and the gambling dens of Las Vegas has attracted much attention, and the same technology is suggested for the short hop between Milwaukee and Chicago where once the legendary *Hiawathas* of the Milwaukee Road stormed in daily steam-hauled grandeur.

Yet another scheme foresees supertrains whisking New Yorkers along the 600km Empire Corridor of the Hudson valley to Montreal. Once there, passengers would be able to change trains for a swift 2hr trip to Toronto on the shore of Lake Ontario at up to 290km/h. This 570km corridor taking in the Canadian capital Ottawa constitutes one of two potential sites for high speed lines in Canada.

The other unites Calgary and Edmonton, the twin cities of Alberta. In the starry eyes of some Albertan politicians the 300km route would stimulate development, but as the combined population of the two cities is not much more than 1 million this was a sure non-starter, and it was officially scrapped in February 1987. For comparison the population in the Montreal–Toronto corridor is around the 7 million mark, still way below the levels that justify high speed railways elsewhere.

Before any of the North American lines materialise several barriers must be conquered. First the ignorance of a generation of middle and upper class North Americans who have grown up in an environment where transport consists entirely of large cars and aircraft must be overcome. So must the cynicism of financial punters (and many senior US railroad officials) who refuse to believe that the shinkansen and the TGV make money. Then there have to be US engineers who know sufficient about high speed railways to be able to build and operate them. The USA, despite all the hurdles, is one of the few places in the world where more high speed trains might just materialise.

## Seoul–Pusan and Rio–São Paulo

Only two other countries have seriously considered high speed trains. By far the more bullish of the two is South Korea where tremendous growth is sustaining a booming economy. The teeming cities of Seoul and Pusan generated 57 million journeys between them in 1985.

In that year Danish consultants Kampsax, Louis Berger of the USA and the Korean Research Institute for Human Settlements completed a major dossier on the potential of a 378km high speed line. The government has been mulling over the contents ever since, but in May 1986 *The Korea Times* reported that the Louise (sic) Berger report had recommended a new line costing $US2,778 million. The Transport Minister Sohn soo-ik was quoted as saying construction of the line was 'inevitable'.

Certainly Korean National Railroad views its 446km existing route between the two cities as a prime candidate for development. In 1985 it offered three inter-city departures an hour in each direction, the fastest being the air-conditioned *Saemaul* trains. Over the years KNR has steadily honed down the Seoul–Pusan times towards a goal of 4hr, which it finally reached in July 1986. In that month a superior

*Saemaul-ho* service with new lightweight coaches and streamlined locomotives was introduced. At first glance they appear to be high speed trains, but the locomotive's angled nose masks a standard General Motors diesel whose top speed is only 150km/h. The *Saemaul-ho* may nonetheless be the harbinger of a Korean shinkansen.

On the basis of the present rail service no-one would ever dream that the Rio de Janeiro–São Paulo corridor has attracted the salesmen of high speed trains. Frankly, the service provided between these two giant cities is a joke. A single day train is allowed a more than leisurely timing for the 500km trip of 8½hr in one direction and over 9hr in the other. Overnight the *Santa Cruz* offers first class sleepers, good service and a diner, but it is a sad relic for Brazil's primary inter-city corridor. The trouble is the competition.

A fleet of ageing Lockheed Electra aircraft shuttles furiously between downtown air terminals in both cities, giving business travellers a 55min inter-city journey. Lesser mortals travel by air-conditioned buses on a 360km four-lane highway, competing for custom with departures at intervals of a few minutes.

The railways are handicapped by heavy freight sharing the same tracks, but the real reason for rail's inability to match other modes was a deliberate decision by the former military government to wind down long distance rail travel. Money was poured into new roads, while the Brazilian airlines provide excellent services for the vast distances. The railways were given the job of shifting heavy freight and commuters, while the main line expresses slumped into decay. I recall a trip in 1981 on a São Paulo Railway express formed of ex-US cars from the 1950s; in my car only three windows were intact.

Such neglect spelt curtains for many of Brazil's long distance services, but in 1985 the change in government brought a different outlook. In 1986 Transport Minister Jose Reinaldo Tavares arrived back from Japan armed with a portfolio of proposals for high speed services. Prominent among these was a proposal for tilting trains that would cut the journey time between São Paulo and Rio to 3hr.

The Federal Railways had toed the previous government's line, but the official change of heart saw their commercial director speaking out in favour of reinvigorating the Rio–São Paulo corridor. Whether apathy, inertia and the nation's burden of foreign debt will ever permit rail to regain a share of the inter-city cake depends on the government's readiness to back talk with cash and action.

A high speed railway is an adventure that needs political commitment. Without that essential ingredient, the plans are fodder for the shredder, the work of dreamers and armchair engineers.

# 15

# ENTER THE ENGLISH ELECTRA

Perhaps the most unlikely entrant in the 300km/h stakes was the English Electra. Until 1986 no-one had expected Britain to put up a contestant – there was no reason to believe that 300km/h would ever be considered by BR or its suppliers. But the Channel Tunnel accord signed by Prime Minister Margaret Thatcher and French President François Mitterrand on January 20 – exactly 11 years after abandonment of the previous project – injected fresh vigour into Britain's railway community.

The Tunnel scheme of the 1980s was a carbon-copy of the 1970s project offering through rail services sharing twin bores with shuttle trains carrying motor vehicles. But there was a significant difference – to conform with the ideology of Britain's Conservative government it was to be privately financed, with no government guarantees to underwrite the operation.

The scheme had been chosen as the most robust of four that varied from a half-baked drive-through road tunnel with trains running in the same bore, put forward at the last minute by shipping and container magnate James Sherwood, to a grandiose and extremely expensive combined bridge and tunnel with fairy-tale islands in mid-Channel.

Revival of the Channel Tunnel had several important consequences. Apart from being a sophisticated railway in its own right, it would plug BR into the European network, opening up dramatic opportunities for inter-city rail travel. It enhanced the prospects of building a third TGV line stretching from Paris to northern France, Brussels and beyond. It was also a catalyst for railway developments in Britain where high speed electric trains from London to Paris and Brussels suddenly became a real possibility.

In the post-APT era the future for high speed electric traction on BR had been unclear, to say the least. From May 1984 the West Coast main line to Glasgow and the northwest offered a handful of 177km/h trains, but further progress had to wait until 27 July when Secretary of State for Transport Nicholas Ridley approved electrification at 25kV 50Hz of the East Coast main line from London to Leeds and Edinburgh at a cost of £306 million. (In fact, the southern end had already been wired as far as Hitchin, leaving 581 route-km from there to Edinburgh and a further 48 from Doncaster to Leeds.) It was the largest electrification project ever authorised in Britain.

BR's submission to invest in the East Coast electrification had assumed that the electric East Coast expresses would be hauled by six-axle Class 89 locomotives, a prototype of which had been ordered in summer 1983.

Class 89 was the first ac main line electric motive power to be ordered since the APT. Its 200km/h maximum speed was no better than the highly successful diesel-powered HSTs, limiting its ability to offer faster journeys on the HST racecourse from Kings Cross to Leeds and Edinburgh. BR anticipated that turning the route over to electric traction would knock a mere 10min off the fastest London–Edinburgh timing and just 6min off the London–Newcastle trip. Under the Department of Transport's investment criteria faster journey times were not the most important item, and BR had justified the £306 million not so much on benefits to the passenger as on energy savings and a healthy reduction in maintenance costs.

Electrification of the East Coast route was badly needed, for the HSTs could not go on for ever. The duty cycle for the Paxman Valenta engines was exceptionally demanding, and their maintenance was a hefty item in the operating bill. In 1986 BR even chose to experiment with replacement engines from Mirrlees, but the Valentas remained the mainstay of BR's 200km/h traction. Their constant punishment led to rashes of failures, but dedicated maintenance staff kept the HSTs in traffic, and they continued to turn in excellent performance. A particularly dramatic run took place in autumn 1985 when BR reintroduced Pullman travel to the East Coast route with the *Tees-Tyne Pullman*.

For the event the Eastern Region turned out a formation of two specially chosen power cars and five MkIII coaches. Hurtling down Stoke Bank, the hallowed ground where *Mallard* had captured the world speed record for steam nearly half a century before, the special touched 145mph (233km/h) according to the cab speedometer, although the official timekeeper on the train calculated the maximum to be 144mph (231.7km/h). The train covered the 433km from Newcastle to Kings Cross in a fabulous time of just under 2hr 20min, a start-to-stop average of 185.8km/h, with the final 161km/h being completed at the stunning average of 190.4km/h.

In the HST, Class 89 had an enormous reputation to live up to. Its six-axle wheel arrangement, however, was not ideal for high speed running. Although it kept the axleload to 17.5 tonnes and unsprung mass was specified at 2.18 tonnes, the distance between the outer axles of each bogie was 4.4 metres – threatening more wear and tear on railhead and wheel flanges than a Bo-Bo; this should however be offset to some extent by the ability of all three axles to 'float' laterally. Thyristor control of the traction motors represented an advance over all other BR ac locomotives bar a lone Class 87 prototype and its Class 90 derivatives, but in many ways the design had already been overtaken. With the long shadow of APT hanging over it, BR had sought in the Class 89 order not to explore the frontiers of technology but to take out an insurance policy. Thus there was no rush to get the Class 89 into traffic, and it did not turn a wheel on BR tracks under its own power until 10 February 1987. By October 1987 it looked as though Class 89 would end up hauling freight.

## Electra order

With the East Coast electrification authorised, BR had more incentive to progress plans for a purpose-built high speed electric. For some time there had been talk of something called InterCity 225 to fill the void left by APT. The designation echoed the marketing name of the HSTs and reflected the proposed top speed, in km/h this time. It was a rather tortuous link so when tenders went out early in 1985 for a new high speed locomotive BR dubbed it Electra. In traction parlance it was simply Class 91.

Three companies were invited to bid for 56 Electras: Britain's General Electric Co (GEC), Brush Electrical Machines of Loughborough – which was building the prototype Class 89 – and Asea of Sweden, to which BR had turned for the APT electrical equipment.

According to InterCity Engineer David Boocock, once BR's 'Mr APT', the Bo-Bo Class 91 'was derived conceptually' from the APT-P power car. There was a certain irony here, for the Class 91 order confirmed once and for all that APT was dead – Electra was being given the job that APT should have done.

The outstanding APT features – fixed formation, articulation, and hydrokinetic brakes – had all vanished, and only one vestige remained – the tilt. But tilting was not envisaged for the new coaches that were to run with the Electras on the relatively straight East Coast main line. BR insisted, however, that a 6° tilt capability was needed

Winners and losers. An AEM–7 'Mighty Mouse' locomotive waits with an original Metroliner EMU at Amtrak's Washington station in October 1980. Six years later the Mighty Mice were given clearance to run at 200km/h on parts of the Northeast Corridor. *Richard Hope*

British Phoenix. The first of British Rail's 240km/h Class 91 Electra locomotives is to be handed over in February 1988 from supplier GEC. This impression was produced by the design consultants in 1986. *DCA Design Consultants*

for new coaches that might be built later for the sinuous West Coast route.

BR announced the winner of the Electra contract on 6 February 1986, less than three weeks after the Lille accord on the Channel Tunnel. For £35 million GEC was to supply 31 Electras for the East Coast main line – BR had persuaded the Department of Transport to convert its submission for Class 89 locomotives to Class 91.

It soon emerged that Class 91 was to have a design capability of 240km/h, although the line speed on the East Coast main line remained officially at 200km/h. But hints of a more bullish policy were confirmed in July 1986 by BR's newly-appointed InterCity Director Dr John Prideaux who revealed that he was planning to clip the London–Edinburgh time to less than 4hr by the time electrification was finished in 1991. This demanded an average speed of 158km/h.

Electra (a name, incidentally, that Prideaux is said not to favour, although he apparently cannot suggest anything better) had a pretty demanding specification. It had to be able to haul or propel in push-pull mode a 10 coach East Coast express grossing 600 tonnes at 225km/h and handle sleeping car or parcels trains loading up to 830 tonnes at 160km/h. The continuous rating was 4,350kW, with weight restricted to 80 tonnes and a limit on the unsprung mass on each axle of 1.7 tonnes.

Because of the push-pull requirement, the Electra has a streamlined nose at one end and a blunt cab at the other; it will normally be matched with a similarly streamlined driving van trailer at the other end of the train. The main transformer is slung below the body to keep the centre of gravity low and help limit roll at high speed.

Separately excited traction motors have the excitation controlled by microprocessors, permitting the motor characteristic to be varied to suit the traction duty, as well as exploiting available adhesion to the maximum.

The Electra's drive improves on that chosen for the APT, which had the motors mounted in the body with the drive through separate transfer and right angle gear boxes connected by long cardan shafts. This arrangement occupied valuable space in the body and had a high centre of gravity. In the Electra the motors are slung at an angle from the body within the bogie frame, driving the axles through short cardan shafts and bogie-mounted bevel gearboxes. Because the motors take up so much space within the bogie, traction and braking forces are transmitted through a low-level Watts linkage.

The cramped space in the bogie also ruled out disc brakes on the axles, so discs have been cunningly mounted on the rear end of the motor shafts. Braking from maximum speed to about 45km/h will be rheostatic, although conventional clasp brakes are also fitted.

Until Easter 1986 Electra was a purely domestic affair. But the Channel Tunnel was already exerting its influence. Since the abandonment of the previous Tunnel, BR and Britain's railway industry had been untouched by the tide of high speed developments sweeping Western Europe. Whether through insularity or xenophobia, some senior BR officials seemed unaware of the TGV's significance for Europe's railways, preferring to denigrate it as an expensive French toy and ignoring SNCF's predictions that all capital and interest will be paid off by the end of the decade.

It is worth recalling that SNCF financed the Fr13.6 billion (1984 values) cost of the Paris–Sud-Est line and its rolling stock by means of loans without any help from the government. In 1985 TGV services earned Fr3.5 billion in revenue for working expenses of Fr1.2 billion. After servicing the original investment, which absorbed Fr1.5 billion, there was a net profit of Fr700 million.

On the other hand, no-one in BR wanted to stir up the new line controversy of 1974. Nor was BR in a position to defend the Tunnel or enthuse too much about its possibilities because it was no longer a national railway project – it was in the hands of a private consortium of banks and civil engineering companies.

It was BR's suppliers who took the initiative. In the 1970s they had been through what can only be described as a British railway recession. A combination of unhelpful government policies, trade union intransigence and ineffective railway management had reduced the railway community to near despair. This culminated at the end of 1981 in the government's refusal to countenance further electrification, resulting in the team that had wired up the so-called Bedpan line between Bedford and London St Pancras being disbanded. Only with the East Coast electrification did the tide begin to turn.

For years no British company had built main line locomotives for export. GEC had contrived to remain in the locomotive manufacturing business, but most of its motive power was assembled outside Britain, notably in South Africa, where it enjoyed a substantial market. Many of these difficulties could be traced back to the 1968 Transport Act which had led to BR building a large share of its own rolling stock through its subsidiary British Rail Engineering Ltd (BREL), leaving private industry to stagnate.

It was the same with coach builders. Only one major manufacturer in the private sector was left in the field: Metro-Cammell of Birmingham. For many years Metro-Cammell had relied on contracts from the London Underground, while a series of orders from Hong Kong kept the company in business in the late 1970s and early 1980s. These orders eventually dried up, and the company's future was staked on winning a contract for the Singapore metro. In a long drawn out and increasingly tense battle Metro-Cammell Chairman Tony Sansome lost to a Japanese consortium in April 1984. Metro-Cammell seemed to be on the verge of giving up.

In 1985 breaks appeared in the clouds. BR won important productivity concessions from its trade unions, and under government pressure began putting new rolling stock contracts out to competitive tender. Metro-Cammell had secured another Hong Kong order as well as a share in a build of diesel multiple-units for BR's cross-country services. BREL was being restructured with a view to privatisation of its manufacturing division.

Brush too was bouncing back. Just as the Channel Tunnel announcement came the Loughborough based company was putting the finishing touches to the first main line electric locomotives that Britain had exported since the late 1960s. These were a batch of 22 Bo-Bo-Bo electrics destined to haul freight on New Zealand Railways.

## Super-Electra

By the start of 1986 this group of four suppliers – GEC, Metro-Cammell, BREL and Brush – was recovering from the famine. Reinvigorated by new contracts, they seized on the Channel Tunnel as a golden opportunity. Pooling experience and resources and taking the Electra and BR's planned MkIV coach as a starting point, they put together a design concept for a 300km/h train to run to mainland Europe.

On 21 March the four met BR, and in the following week the Railway Industry Association – which for years had been content to take a backseat – called a press conference at GEC's London offices. GEC and BREL outlined plans for a 14 car train powered by a brace of Super-Electras. A locomotive marshalled at each end of the formation would have a continuous rating of 5,000kW at 200km/h. Up to 1,000 passengers would be accommodated in a tourist class version of the train with what GEC's Technical Director described as 'distributed vending'. A more luxurious variant boasted two catering cars and 600 seats.

It was all brave talk, and the Railway Industry Association press release even went so far as to say that 'the UK consortium is confident that its proposals have a significant technological advantage over other schemes so far suggested'.

True, the Super-Electra was of considerable technical interest. It featured the same novel transmission as the BR Electra, but coupled it with three-phase asynchronous induction motors. Three-phase drives had been largely ignored by BR, although its own Research & Development Division had designed a three-phase motor and installed it inside a hollow axle in the mid-1970s. Later, the concept was further developed by GEC, but this ingenious idea unfortunately did not succeed, apparently because the power output was only about two thirds of what it was expected to be.

GEC kept the three-phase technique alive in Britain and in 1985 the company supplied about 250 sets of three-phase drive equipment to North America, mainly for the linear-motored *Skytrain* automated Metro that opened in Vancouver in January 1986.

GEC also pointed to experience with the various power electronics that it had in mind for the Super-Electra, including high power GTO thyristors. In 1985–86 it was supplying GTOs for locomotives in South Africa, for the Docklands Light Railway which opened in August 1987 in East London, and even for the Class 319 electric multiple-units with which BR launches the 'ThamesLink' service through London's reopened Snow Hill tunnel between Blackfriars and Farringdon in May 1988.

The use of GTOs for high power traction control was especially significant for the Super-Electra. Thanks to the absence of commutating circuits, valuable space was released for other components. Not only would the Super-Electra have to sport enough power to whisk its train up to 300km/h, but it would also have to house an array of electrical equipment to cope with Western Europe's bewildering range of traction power supplies. GEC was confident that it could accept five; 750V dc third rail on British Rail's Southern Region, 25kV 50Hz overhead in northern France (and possibly north of London in Great Britain), 3kV dc overhead in Belgium, 1.5kV dc overhead in the Netherlands, and 15kV 16⅔Hz in West Germany.

BR was caught by surprise by the Super-Electra proposals, but it did agree to lend its support to the promoters. There were many outstanding questions, not least being where to test a prototype Super-Electra at its design speed of 300km/h.

The consortium had not ducked such an important question and suggested that a section of the East Coast main line be fettled up to permit trials at 300km/h. This would mean major attention to the track, almost certainly with realignment to ease curves, special catenary and possibly power supply arrangements, modifications to the signalling, and so on. There is also the difficulty of fitting in paths for 300km/h test trains on BR's second busiest inter-city route.

Meantime the French were assuming, not unreasonably, that any high speed train that ran through the Channel Tunnel would be a bantam version of the TGV conforming to BR's restrictive loading gauge. They were entitled to some incredulity over the Super-Electra. It had taken over nine years for SNCF to perfect the technology of TGV 001 to the stage where electric TGVs were carrying fare-paying passengers, and another eight look set to go by before the step up to 300km/h is made in 1989. For Britain to commission a proven train able to run day-in day-out at 300km/h in 1993 seemed unprecedentedly ambitious.

There was one obvious problem. The TGV axleload is limited to 17 tonnes, and this was enshrined in the specification for cross-Channel trains that SNCF and BR had agreed by early 1987. Although the unsprung mass on the Electra was only 1.7 tonnes, radical redesign would be needed to meet the axleload limit.

When the British Channel Tunnel train was floated, neither the locomotive nor the coaches existed. The first East Coast Electra was not due to be finished until February 1988 (10 are being built ahead of the main batch so that any bugs can be ironed out before the full fleet is commissioned), and tenders for BR's first MkIV coaches were not placed until Christmas 1986.

While the French might regard Electra's ancestry as a little dubious, that of the MkIV coaches is impeccable. BR'S MkIII coaches have been running at 200km/h for over 10 years, and in terms of value for money and seats per tonne they are unsurpassed by any comparable design in the world.

The 283 MkIVs ordered from Metro-Cammell for £83 million will run on a bogie developed by SIG of Switzerland. It was to have been BREL's T4 or Cheetah design which was road tested at high speed in November 1986 when a special set of cars marshalled between a pair of HST power cars was flogged up to 233km/h. This constituted an official world record for diesel traction – the similar speed reached by the *Tees-Tyne Pullman* in autumn 1985 was not measured with the same exactitude as on the Cheetah test train. Sadly the T4 was not perfected in time and BR chose the Swiss alternative.

But breaking records is one thing. The acid test of commercial service is another. On the date it was proposed, the Super-Electra was a paper tiger, designed to force the French not to ignore their British partners in the competition for design of the cross-Channel trains.

# 16

# THE INTERNATIONAL DIMENSION

Apart from the embryonic TGV–Est scheme mentioned in Chapter 13 all the high speed lines considered up to now have been purely domestic. Even in the closely-knit framework of the European Community, domestic rail traffic nearly always takes priority over international services. Frontiers are psychological as well as physical barriers, and nowhere is this more true than on the northern side of the English Channel.

Building a high speed railway is in itself a major undertaking, but building one across a frontier more than doubles the complexity. Not for nothing did SNCF shy away from Robert Geais' proposal for a high speed line from Paris to Lille in the 1960s (Chapter 7), for to be worthwhile it had to continue to Brussels and under the Channel to London. It was dealt a fatal blow by the British cancellation of the last Channel Tunnel project in 1975.

The idea did not surface again until the early 1980s. It was one of several schemes like TGV–Est which mushroomed in the wake of the launch of the Paris–Sud-Est line. Known as TGV–Nord, it began as a high speed link from Paris to Brussels, from where trains would continue through Aachen into West Germany to meet the DB's Intercity network at Cologne. The Channel Tunnel was once more being warmed up, lending encouragement to the promoters of the new line.

Tentative route and traffic studies were carried out, and on 18 July 1983 France's Transport Minister Charles Fiterman met his counterparts from Belgium and West Germany, Herman de Croo and Dr Werner Dollinger in Paris to thrash out some firm ideas. The three set up a working party to report on technical, economic, legal and social implications.

TGV–Nord promised to transform the transport geography of northern Europe. Assuming 300km/h running, journey time between the Belgian and French capitals would be a mere 1hr 15min, and the

Paris–Cologne time would be more than halved from the *Parsifal*'s 1986 timing of 5hr 15min to just 2hr 30min. Lille, home of the world's first driverless metro, would be just under 1hr from Paris, with the Tunnel portal only a few minutes away. Supposing a time through the Tunnel of about 25min, London bound high speed trains would reach their destination in little more than 3hr from Paris.

The 3hr timing compares well with the best city centre to city centre air journey. A whole hour has to be allowed for the haul out from central Paris to Roissy Charles de Gaulle airport where at least 30min is needed for check-in; flying time occupies another hour, while baggage collection at Heathrow may take 30min or more; the last leg into central London can easily swallow a further 60min.

During 1985 a head of steam favouring TGV–Nord was worked up in France by the socialist government. In Belgium Communications Minister de Croo lent his weight to the project, while the idea of a spur to Amsterdam brought the Dutch in as active partners.

Meeting again in January 1986, the ministers endorsed the principle of the scheme, which entailed building at least 400 and possibly as much as 550km of new line. Of this total, 210km would be in France and 234km in Belgium. Raising the £2bn to fund it was the thorniest problem, and the trio of ministers canvassed a range of financial scenarios. One suggestion was to set up an international finance company able to draw on public and private funds in what the French referred to as a *montage financier*.

But the pace soon slackened in France with the arrival of the Chirac administration which did not have the same enthusiasm as its predecessors – Charles Fiterman's hope that 'it would be a single project of European dimensions which might well form the basis for a whole network of high speed lines' was not shared by his right-wing successors.

It was evident from the start that the busiest part of the line would be the western end with traffic between Paris, Brussels and London. Chirac's government estimated that inter-capital flows would total 22.4 million passengers a year, with nearly another 10 million between Paris and northern France. East of Brussels only 7 to 8 million passengers a year are expected, giving rise to fears by the Belgians that TGV–Nord would simply be a domestic French TGV route from Paris to Lille and the Tunnel portal, with a branch to Brussels tacked on.

Belgian politics are influenced by the rivalry between Flemings and Walloons. Effectively that means investment must be split equally between the two areas of the country, a factor which complicates any plan such as TGV–Nord. Pressure was building up for the line to bring tangible benefits for inter-city journeys within Belgium, and not least among those who favoured this view was the 28 year old President of Belgian Railways, Didier Reynders, appointed in October 1986. Leaks about plans to expropriate land had in the meantime upset de Croo's applecart, and at one time he found himself defending the project against members of his own liberal party.

It is not only politics that influence the course of events. Not least among the other factors is national pride, to say nothing of rules and regulations which govern the operation of different railways. I happened to visit Brussels in mid-1986, and from there I continued by train into Germany to see for myself the route over which high speed trains might one day cruise to Cologne.

Boarding a train from Paris to Cologne in Brussels I noticed that it had been hauled from the French capital by a four-current locomotive specially built so that it could accept the power supply of the three countries concerned. The train was scheduled for a 15min layover in Brussels–Midi, which was explained by the locomotive being exchanged for an identical machine owned by the Belgian Railways. I innocently assumed this was going to haul my train through to Cologne, but I was wrong. The Belgian machine travelled under the 3kV catenary to the frontier at Aachen, where it was replaced by a third locomotive, this one belonging to the DB.

Here was a case where the technical achievement of building four-current locomotives had been laid to waste by national differences, and this absurd practice had been going on for years. Happily the launch of Euro-City services in May 1987 was accompanied by an agreement to make better use of the not inconsiderable pool of poly-current motive power in Europe, which was a long-overdue step in international co-operation at grass-roots level.

Although the Channel Tunnel boosted the traffic projections – it also brought Britain in as a rather lukewarm partner – in autumn 1986 French Transport Minister Jacques Douffiagues revealed that TGV–Nord only just met the minimum 9 per cent rate of return for railway investment in France if Channel Tunnel traffic was included. His statement bound the Channel Tunnel and TGV–Nord projects together.

There were certain similarities between the two schemes, including pressure for TGV–Nord to be financed by private investment, a line of thinking which gathered pace as soon as the British government became involved. It was however unacceptable to the Belgians, Dutch and Germans because there was no chance of the lines east of Brussels being built on a strict commercial basis. In France, however, the Chirac government was by September 1987 virtually certain of private finance for its share of the route, and even the Belgians seemed to be coming round to the same way of thinking.

Enthusiasm for TGV–Nord did not diminish. Industry and local chambers of commerce in northern France were anxious to profit from the new line. Lille gained a foretaste of high speed service when a weekday TGV to and from Lyons was introduced in 1984. This was successful enough for SNCF to add another working in 1986. In September of that year Normandy too was granted its own TGV direct to Lyons.

Towns potentially on the route of TGV–Nord clamoured for the new line to pass close enough to give them their own station, and Amiens in particular campaigned to be on the line of route which looked as though it would follow the A1 *autoroute* further east. Douffiagues responded to these shrill appeals by ruling that the route could not zig-zag from Roissy airport (where the new line is likely to start) to Soissons, St Quentin and back to Amiens. Nonetheless he conceded that a kink to serve Amiens was not ruled out, although this would impose time and cost penalties.

With so many uncertainties, it was hardly surprising that when the European Council of Ministers met on 22 December 1986 in The Hague they put off doing anything further until another meeting in October or November 1987.

About the only concrete decision taken in The Hague was rejection of a maglev option based on German Transrapid technology. This had only been included in the dossiers for the sake of form, because it had in practice already been ruled out on grounds of incompatibility, besides which the incompleted Emsland test track was hardly sufficient evidence that a full-blown maglev transport system could be built and operated at known costs. In 1984 a proposed 380km/h maglev line from Paris to Cologne was costed at nearly half as much again as a 240km/h railway, and even with such a high speed it had a negative rate of return.

On 29 July 1987 the French and British premiers ratified the Channel Tunnel Treaty after Tunnel legislation had cleared the British parliament for the first time in history. This paved the way for Eurotunnel, the Anglo–French grouping which in 1986 won the 55 year concession to build and operate the Tunnel, to go ahead. Major construction work is due to get under way at the British worksite at Shakespeare cliff in December 1987 – assuming that Eurotunnel's £750m equity issue succeeds the previous month. Earlier in the year BR and its continental partners had dusted off plans for high speed services between London, Paris and Brussels, and design proposals for a fleet of 40 to 50 trains able to run at 300km/h were invited during the summer. On 1 October 1987 a consortium of four British, three French and two Belgian companies was announced to build them.

Eight days later French Prime Minister Jacques Chirac announced the go-ahead for TGV-Nord, with links round Paris to the Sud-Est and Atlantique lines. On top of that, the extension of TGV–Sud-Est past Lyon, was agreed, and Chirac even affirmed that plans would proceed for TGV-Est to Strasbourg. Contrary to expectations 'it is the SNCF that will finance this network', said Chirac. On 26 October the European ministers of transport gave their formal approval to the TGV-Nord scheme.

With the Treaty safely signed, BR was able to explore once again options for high speed running between London and the Tunnel, and it has undertaken to submit proposals for raising speed and capacity to the transport minister by June 1988. These could include Britain's first dedicated high speed route, which under the Thatcher regime could well be privately financed.

In the TGV–Nord report presented to the European Council of Ministers before Christmas 1986 specific rolling stock requirements were suggested for different route scenarios. Assuming a new line from Paris to Brussels with trains running over existing lines to Amsterdam and Cologne, a fleet of 76 four-current trains would be needed, with 50 more to run through the Channel Tunnel. These proposals were refined during 1987, and SNCF revealed in August that it envisaged a fleet of 64 sets costing Fr6bn. (The French part of the new line had a price tag of around Fr10bn.) 29 sets would be dual-current for working Paris–Lille–Brussels services, 14 would have four-current capability for running through to Cologne, and 21 would be equipped to run in Britain. BR confirmed that 42 jointly-owned trains were needed to carry nearly 16 million passengers a year to and from the Continent; a 'responsibility split' of 18 each for the British and French and 6 for the Belgians was anticipated.

Whatever British industry or BR officials like to say there is no doubt that the London–Paris trains of the future will owe their existence to the extraordinary European interest in high speed rail travel generated by the superlative achievement of the Paris–Sud-Est TGV line. It is a remarkable fact that when the TGV-Atlantique line is in business something like two thirds of France's population will have access to TGVs. When the world's first 300km/h railway is inaugurated in 1989, Paris Montparnasse will be as good a venue as any to celebrate 200 years of the French revolution. And, Eurotunnel permitting, the British can invade France at 300km/h in 1993.

# APPENDIX

## Notable speed records at 100mph or more

| Date | Country | Location | Speed km/h | Speed mph | Train | Remarks | |
|---|---|---|---|---|---|---|---|
| *9 May 1893* | USA | New York Central | 165.4 | 102.8 | 999, Empire SX | unauthenticated | s |
| *11 May 1893* | USA | New York Central | 181.0 | 112.5 | 999, Empire SX | unauthenticated | s |
| *1901* | Germany | Marienfelde–Zossen | 162.5 | 101.0 | S&H loco | world record | e |
| *6 Oct 1903* | Germany | Marienfelde–Zossen | 202.7 | 126.0 | S&H railcar | world record | e |
| *23 Oct 1903* | Germany | Marienfelde–Zossen | 206.8 | 128.5 | S&H railcar | world record | e |
| *27 Oct 1903* | Germany | Marienfelde–Zossen | 210.2 | 130.6 | AEG railcar | world record | e |
| *1903* | GB | Hullavington–Lit Somerfd | 193.1 | 120.0 | 2903 Lady of Lyons | unauthenticated | s |
| *9 May 1904* | GB | Exeter–Taunton | 164.6 | 102.3 | City of Truro | disputed | s |
| *11 June 1905* | USA | New York–Chicago | 204.5 | 127.1 | E2 4–4–2 7002 | unauthenticated | s |
| *May 1927* | USA | Washington–New York | 185.1 | 115.0 | E6s 4–4–2 460 | unauthenticated | s |
| *21 June 1931* | Germany | Ludwigslust–Wittenberge | 230.2 | 143.0 | Schienenzeppelin | world record | prop |
| *19 Dec 1932* | Germany | Berlin-Hamburg | 165.0 | 102.5 | VT877 railcar | diesel record | d |
| *26 May 1934* | USA | Denver-Lincoln | 181.0 | 112.5 | Pioneer Zephyr | diesel record | d |
| *30 Nov 1934* | GB | Grantham–Peterborough | 161.0 | 100.0 | Flying Scotsman | LNER trial run | s |
| *5 Mar 1935* | GB | Grantham–Peterborough | 173.8 | 108.0 | Papyrus A3 | LNER trial run | s |
| *8 May 1935* | USA | Milwaukee-New Lisbon | 181.0 | 112.5 | Milwaukee 4–4–2 | Hiawatha trial | s |
| *27 Sep 1935* | GB | Kings Cross–Peterborough | 181.0 | 112.5 | A4 Silver Link | Silver Jubilee demo | s |
| *17 Feb 1936* | Germany | Ludwigslust–Wittenberge | 205.0 | 127.4 | Leipzig railcar | diesel record | d |
| *11 May 1936* | Germany | Neustadt an der Dosse | 200.4 | 124.5 | 05.002 4–6–4 | DR demonstration | s |
| *29 Jun 1937* | GB | Madeley–Crewe | 181.0 | 112.5 | 4–6–2 6220 | LMS press run | s |
| *3 Jul 1938* | GB | Grantham–Peterborough | 202.8 | 126.0 | A4 Mallard 4–6–2 | steam record | s |
| *23 Jun 1939* | Germany | Hamburg–Berlin | 215.0 | 133.6 | Kruckenberg set | diesel record | d |
| *20 Jul 1939* | Italy | Bologna-Milan | 203.0 | 126.1 | ETR200 | FS demonstration | e |
| *21 Feb 1954* | France | Dijon-Beaune | 243.0 | 151.0 | CC7121 | world record | e |
| *26 Mar 1955* | France | Lamothe-Morcenx | 276.0 | 171.5 | BB9004 | world record | e |
| *28 Mar 1955* | France | Lamothe-Morcenx | 326.0 | 202.6 | CC7107 | world record | e |
| *29 Mar 1955* | France | Lamothe-Morcenx | 331.0 | 205.7 | BB9004 | world record | e |
| *23/24 Jul 1966* | USA | Bryan, Ohio | 295.8 | 183.8 | Budd railcar | Jet powered | j |

## Notable speed records at 100mph or more

| Date | Country | Location | Speed km/h | Speed mph | Train | Remarks | |
|---|---|---|---|---|---|---|---|
| *Oct 1970/May 1971* | GB | Watford–Bletchley | 207.6 | 129.0 | E3173 | Trials for HST | e |
| *20 May 1972* | Spain | Azuqueca–Guadalajara | 222.0 | 137.9 | 353–005, Talgo | diesel record | d |
| *8 Dec 1972* | France | Lamothe–Morcenx | 318.0 | 197.6 | TGV 001 | gas turbine | gt |
| *6 Jun 1973* | GB | York–Darlington | 210.8 | 131.0 | HST prototype | British record | d |
| *12 Jun 1973* | GB | Northallerton–Thirsk | 230.5 | 143.2 | HST prototype | diesel record | d |
| *14 Aug 1974* | USA | Pueblo, Colorado | 410.0 | 254.7 | Garrett car | on 1,435mm gauge track | |
| *10 Mar 1976* | Canada | CP line E of Montreal | 208.0 | 129.25 | LRC | Canadian record | d |
| *3 Aug 1975* | GB | Uffington–Goring | 243.5 | 151.3 | APT–E | British record | gt |
| *10 Aug 1975* | GB | Uffington–Goring | 245.1 | 152.3 | APT–E | British record | gt |
| *4 May 1978* | Spain | Alcazar de San Juan | 230.0 | 142.9 | 353–001, Talgo | Spanish record | d |
| *end 1978* | S Africa | Midway–Westonaria | 245.0 | 152.2 | Class 6E | 1,067mm record | e |
| *7 Dec 1979* | Japan | Oyama test track | 319.0 | 198.2 | Series 961 set | Japanese record | e |
| *12 Dec 1979* | GB | Beattock–Lockerbie | 249.4 | 155.0 | APT–P formation | British record | e |
| *20 Dec 1979* | GB | Beattock–Lockerbie | 257.5 | 160.0 | APT–P formation | British record | e |
| *25 Feb 1981* | France | near Tonnerre | 371.0 | 230.5 | TGV set ‘33’ | world record | e |
| *26 Feb 1981* | France | Moulins en Tonnerrois | 380.4 | 236.4 | TGV set 16 | world record | e |
| *17 Apr 1984* | W Germany | Augsburg–Donauwörth | 265.0 | 164.7 | 120,001 | German record | e |
| *14 Jun 1985* | W Germany | Rheda–Oelde | 283.0 | 175.8 | 103,003 | German record | e |
| *25 Nov 1985* | W Germany | Rheda–Oelde | 323.0 | 200.7 | ICE set | unofficial | e |
| *26 Nov 1985* | W Germany | Rheda–Oelde | 317.0 | 197.0 | ICE set | German record | e |
| *23 Sep 1986* | France | TGV line | 356.3 | 221.4 | TGV Set 10 | Synchronous motored | e |
| *9 Nov 1986* | GB | York–Darlington | 233.2 | 144.9 | HST set | diesel record | d |
| *17 Nov 1986* | W Germany | Burgsinn-Hohe Wart | 345.0 | 214.4 | ICE set | German record | e |
| | | **Non-railway vehicles** | | | | | |
| *22 Jan 1969* | France | Limours–Gometz | 422.0 | 262.2 | Aérotrain vehicle | rocket assisted | |
| *4 Mar 1974* | France | Orléans test track | 428.0 | 265.9 | Aérotrain Orléans | 250–80 | |
| *19 Feb 1976* | W Germany | Manching test track | 401.3 | 249.4 | Komet maglev sled | steam rocket power | |
| *21 Dec 1979* | Japan | Miyazaki test track | 517.0 | 321.3 | JNR ML500 car | unmanned maglev | |
| *12 Dec 1985* | W Germany | Emsland test track | 355.0 | 220.6 | Transrapid 06 | manned maglev | |
| *4 Feb 1987* | Japan | Miyazaki test track | 400.0 | 248.5 | MLU 001 | manned maglev | |

s=*steam*, d=*diesel*, e=*electric*, gt=*gas turbine*, j=*jet propelled*, prop=*propeller driven*

# INDEX

# INDEX